A Practical Guide to Teaching ICT in the Secondary School

This practical and ɑ   hers as they
develop their basic t   derstanding
for teaching. Newly   .

A Practical Guide t   ɪble research
concerning student   ɪ on the key
pedagogical issues ɪ

- managing thɪ
- developing p   conceptions
- different way   blematic.

It provides a wealtɪ   vant theory,
which have been dɪ   vith student
teachers. These act   ɪrformance.
Photocopiable planɪ   ɔles of good
practice and a range

The book has beɪ   *ndary School*
(also published by R   ɪsic teaching
skills covered in tha   ɪcessfully as
a stand-alone text. It   ɔwn or with
others, or by school-ɪ   elop and/or
reinforce their undeɪ   ach ICT.

Steve Kennewell is   ɪre he is ICT
Coordinator and Co   ɪ PGCE ICT
Secondary Course Leader at Keele University, UK. **Anthony Edwards** is Head of ICT in the Education Deanery at Liverpool Hope University, UK. **Michael Hammond** is Secondary PGCE Course Leader ICT and Director of Research Students at the University of Warwick, UK. **Cathy Wickens** is Senior Lecturer in IT at the School of Education, University of Brighton, UK.

Routledge Teaching Guides
Series Editors: Susan Capel and Marilyn Leask

Other titles in the series:

A Practical Guide to Teaching Physical Education in the Secondary School
Edited by *Susan Capel, Peter Breckon and Jean O'Neill*.

A Practical Guide to Teaching History in the Secondary School
Edited by *Martin Hunt*

A Practical Guide to Teaching Modern Foreign Languages in the Secondary School
Edited by *Norbert Pachler and Ana Redondo*

A Practical Guide to Teaching Citizenship in the Secondary School
Edited by *Liam Gearon*

These Practical Guides have been designed as companions to **Learning to Teach (subject) in the Secondary School**. For information on the Routledge Teaching Guides series please visit our website at www.routledge.com/education.

A Practical Guide to Teaching ICT in the Secondary School

Edited by Steve Kennewell, Andrew Connell, Anthony Edwards, Michael Hammond and Cathy Wickens

Routledge
Taylor & Francis Group

LONDON AND NEW YORK

First published 2007 by Routledge
2 Park Square, Milton Park, Abingdon, Oxon, OX14 4RN

Simultaneously published in the USA and Canada
by Routledge
270 Madison Ave, New York, NY 10016

Routledge is an imprint of the Taylor & Francis Group, an informa business

© 2007 Edited by Steve Kennewell, Andrew Connell, Anthony Edwards,
Cathy Wickens and Michael Hammond

Typeset in Palatino and Frutiger by
Keystroke, 28 High Street, Tettenhall, Wolverhampton
Printed and bound in Great Britain by
MPG Books Ltd, Bodmin

British Library Cataloguing in Publication Data
A catalogue record for this book is available from the British Library

Library of Congress Cataloging in Publication Data
A catalog record for this book has been requested

ISBN10: 0–415–40299–9 (pbk)
ISBN10: 0–203–96260–5 (ebk)

ISBN13: 978–0–415–40299–6 (pbk)
ISBN13: 978–0–203–96260–2 (ebk)

Contents

Contributors

Andrew Connell now works at Keele University as PCGE ICT Secondary Course Leader and Learning & Development Coordinator. He has been Associate Director of PGCE Secondary and PGCE ICT Secondary Course Leader at Liverpool Hope University, and Head of ICT and Business in a school in Stoke-on-Trent.

Lynne Dagg is a Senior Lecturer in ICT Education at the University of Sunderland. Prior to this, Lynne worked as an ICT teacher in a variety of Secondary and Further Education establishments. She is active in the British Computer Society.

Phil Duggan is Curriculum Leader for PGCE Applied Subjects at Liverpool John Moores University with specific responsibility for the Applied ICT route. Prior to this he was a local authority KS3 strategy adviser for ICT having been a subject leader in a school for several years.

Anthony Edwards is currently Head of ICT in the Education Deanery at Liverpool Hope University. He has worked in a variety of educational settings in the UK and abroad. His research interests include creativity and new technologies and the application of e-learning.

Michael Hammond coordinates the secondary ICT PGCE course at the University of Warwick and has written widely on teaching ICT as well as teaching with ICT. He has carried out research into the professional development of teachers and has written *Next Steps in Teaching*, also published by Routledge.

Ian Hughes is Head of ICT and ICT Coordinator at Bishop Gore Comprehensive School, Swansea, and teaches on the ICT PGCE course at Swansea School of Education. He contributed to *Learning to Teach ICT in the Secondary School* for Routledge.

Steve Kennewell is the course leader for the ICT PGCE course at Swansea School of Education. He has directed a number of research projects concerning ICT in education, and published extensively including *Developing the ICT-Capable School*, *Learning to Teach ICT in the Secondary School*, and *Meeting the Standards for Using ICT in Secondary Teaching* for Routledge.

Martyn Lawson is a Principal Lecturer in the Faculty of Education at St Martin's College Lancaster. He has been Course Leader for the Secondary ICT PGCE Course for the past four years and now coordinates the provision of all Secondary ITE for St Martin's. Before moving into the HE sector, he was head of ICT in a secondary school in North Yorkshire.

Jude Slama teaches ICT at Plantsbrook school where she is acting head of department. She teaches one day a week on the secondary ICT PGCE course at the University of Warwick. She has a special interest in leading action research projects with student teachers and has carried out her own project on the assessment of ICT.

Neil Stanley is currently Curriculum Leader Undergraduate (Secondary) programmes at Liverpool John Moores University and leads the two-year IT programmes (PGCE and undergraduate). He is the Reviews Editor for Computer Education, the Naace Journal, and contributed to *Learning to Teach ICT in the Secondary School* for Routledge.

Geoff White spent some twenty-five years teaching in schools, mainly computing and ICT, and is now a Senior Lecturer at Bath Spa University. He is the Course Leader for their PGCE in Secondary ICT and is active in the British Computer Society.

Cathy Wickens is a Senior Lecturer in Information Technology Education at the School of Education, University of Brighton, where she runs a large well-established Secondary PGCE and two-year BA IT course. She is also course leader for a four-year BA (Hons) Key Stage 2/3 course which has four different subject specialisms including IT.

John Woollard is a lecturer in Information Technology Education at the School of Education, University of Southampton. He has been a specialist in Special Educational Needs, and his research focus is pedagogy and the teaching of difficult concepts in and with computers.

Series Editors' Introduction

This practical and accessible workbook is part of a series of textbooks for student teachers. It complements and extends the popular textbook entitled *Learning to Teach in the Secondary School: A Companion to School Experience*, as well as the subject-specific textbook *Learning to Teach ICT in the Secondary School*. We anticipate that you will want to use this book in conjunction with these other books.

Teaching is rapidly becoming a more research- and evidence-informed profession. We have used research and professional evidence about what makes good practice to underpin the 'Learning to Teach in the Secondary School' series and these practical workbooks. Both the generic and subject-specific book in the series provide theoretical, research and professional evidence-based advice and guidance to support you as you focus on developing aspects of your teaching or your pupils' learning as you progress through your initial teacher education course and beyond. Although the generic and subject-specific books include some case studies and tasks to help you consider the issues, the practical application of material is not their major focus. That is the role of this book.

This book aims to reinforce your understanding of aspects of your teaching, support you in aspects of your development as a teacher and your teaching and enable you to analyse your success as a teacher in maximising pupils' learning by focusing on practical applications. The practical activities in this book can be used in a number of ways. Some activities are designed to be undertaken by you individually, others as a joint task in pairs and yet others as group work working with, for example, other student teachers or a school- or university-based tutor. Your tutor may use the activities with a group of student teachers. The book has been designed so that you can write directly into it.

In England, new ways of working for teachers are being developed through an initiative remodelling the school workforce. This may mean that you have a range of colleagues to support in your classroom. They also provide an additional resource on which you can draw. In any case, you will, of course, need to draw on additional resources to support your development and the *Learning to Teach in the Secondary School*, 4th edition website (http://www.routledge.com/textbooks/0415363926) lists key websites for Scotland, Wales, Northern Ireland and England. For example, key websites relevant to teachers in England include the Teacher Training Resource Bank (www.ttrb.ac.uk). Others include: www.teachernet.gov.uk which is part of the DfES schools web initiative; www.becta.org.uk, which has ICT resources; and www.qca.org.uk which is the Qualifications and Curriculum Authority website.

We do hope that this practical workbook will be useful in supporting your development as a teacher.

Susan Capel
Marilyn Leask
May 2006

Acknowledgements

The editors would like to acknowledge the support of ITTE, the Association for IT in Teacher Education, in producing this book. We would also like to thank all the teachers, whether named or anonymous, whether experienced or trainee teachers, whose work contributed to the case studies included throughout the book.

We are grateful, too, to the following organisations for permission to include photos:

IMM Studios, Canada
Creative Learning Systems, New Zealand
Swavesey Village College, Cambridgeshire.

Introduction

This book is designed to provide practical guidance and ideas to support trainee teachers of ICT, along with their higher education and school-based tutors/mentors. It will also be of value to qualified teachers who need to develop their teaching of ICT as a subject.

It links to the first book written specifically for this readership, *Learning to Teach ICT in the Secondary School* (also edited by Steve Kennewell), and to *Learning to Teach in the Secondary School: A Companion to School Experience* (edited by Susan Capel, Marilyn Leask and Tony Turner). It addresses in detail many aspects of teaching that are introduced in the previous books, and suggests significant new ideas. It particularly supplements the existing texts by providing a range of activities, based on tried-and-tested strategies, designed to support student teachers' development in aspects of their teaching. These include case studies, examples of pupils' work and examples of existing good practice. This book provides a range of reference and resources associated with each chapter, including photcopiable materials. Furthermore, it gives advice about selection of resources from the plethora available on the web and elsewhere.

In order to ensure that the content is well matched to students' needs, the Association for IT in Teacher Education (ITTE) has been involved from the outset, and all the authors are members of ITTE concerned with specialist ICT courses, together with teachers from their partner schools. The authors are at the leading edge of research into the teaching and learning of ICT as a subject, and the material draws on the best available information concerning student teachers' needs and approaches to learning. The case studies and resources have been developed from the authors' own teaching and experience, which covers nine successful secondary ICT initial teacher training courses.

The book focuses on the key pedagogical issues which arise during school experience, such as:

- planning units of work;
- managing the class and learning environment;
- developing pupils' understanding of important concepts;
- using assessment to improve students' learning and your own teaching;
- finding and implementing new approaches to the National Curriculum;
- strategies for incorporating new technologies as they emerge.

Practical activities are at the heart of the approach, promoting strategic thinking as well as trying to address 'how to' issues. The tasks will stimulate you to seek evidence to support developments in practice, either from your own experiences of teaching or from your reading, and will guide your reflection on the evidence. The book adopts the view that skills, knowledge and understanding in teaching ICT will only be acquired over time, and that a correct answer is not always available. The resources may be used by student teachers individually or in groups, and the resources can be used by tutors/mentors with a group of student teachers. The book has been designed to be written in directly and so provide a useful record.

It is structured in three parts. Part 1 deals with the practicalities of planning, organising, assessing and evaluating your teaching. It will be valuable during your early experiences, but covers the ideas in sufficient depth to be of value throughout your initial training course and into the first year of teaching. Part 2 provides a fresh look at the curriculum, showing how the statutory requirements can be taught using different perspectives which take account of more recent thinking about curriculum requirements. Its structure in terms of Exploration, Prediction, Communication and Creativity is designed to help you motivate learners who are increasingly confident and experienced users of ICT by the time they reach secondary school. Part 3 focuses on your professional learning, from early perceptions at the start of training through to the planning of your Continuing Professional Development during your career in teaching. It will help you to build your pedagogical knowledge during the inevitable frustrations and setbacks of a new career.

The chapters are not designed to be read in sequence, and many cross-references are provided within the text to help you link the key ideas found in different parts. There are also many references to the other linked texts, where these provide supplementary and alternative material. There is a website at (http://www.routledge.com/textbooks/9780415402996) where you can find up-to-date links to web pages referred to in the text, the planning templates from Appendix A, together with links to further resources as they are developed.

Part 1   Preparing to teach ICT: planning, implementation and evaluation

This section aims to provide the busy ICT teacher with practical advice, and guidance on the key areas of planning, resource management, assessment and the 'Learning and Teaching Cycle'. It does not need to be followed in the order presented, nor does it necessarily have to be read from start to finish, though we hope that you will do so.

Chapter 1 deals with the need for planning, recognising that there are different kinds of planning techniques, and with understanding how to plan an ICT lesson. It particularly focuses on common mistakes made in planning ICT lessons, the key questions to ask when planning ICT lessons and the need to plan for ICT coursework.

Chapter 2 considers a variety of matters that affect the success of your plans when you come to implement them. There are many factors which have an impact on the quality of teaching and learning, including welfare factors, the physical environment, classroom layout, computer systems layout, working patterns, resource organisation, and other adults in the classroom. These organisational factors are covered in some detail.

Assessment has a particularly important influence on learning, as well as providing information that you can use to improve your teaching. Chapter 3 discusses what we mean by assessment, the different types of assessment techniques, the need for structured assessment based on learning objectives, and outcomes that can be assessed. It provides guidance in developing practical strategies to help you collect evidence and judge pupil progress, including the important role of moderation.

Chapter 4 focuses on evaluation and the cyclical approach to developing your teaching skills. We discuss what evaluation is and why we evaluate, and provide detailed advice concerning how to evaluate lessons and longer-term planning.

Chapter 1

Planning ICT learning and teaching

ANDREW CONNELL AND ANTHONY EDWARDS

INTRODUCTION

In this first chapter, we look at the meaning and importance of planning, and consider various techniques and the terminology used in planning lessons. We focus particularly on the common mistakes made in planning ICT lessons and the key questions to ask when planning ICT lessons.

By the end of this chapter you should be able to:

- understand the need for planning;
- understand how to plan an ICT lesson;
- understand the need to plan for ICT coursework.

WHY PLAN?

All good teachers need to plan carefully. Poor planning leads to poor teaching and learning. At the beginning of your career in teaching you will plan extensively because you have to learn the process and because your qualification demands it.

There is a place for using your instincts, but they should not be relied upon. Indeed, 'Great lessons do not just happen and they are not a product of good luck. Great lessons are a product of great planning, plus a little bit of inspiration and a tiny amount of good fortune' (Elliot, 2004). In other words, if you want to teach well, then you have to put the effort in to plan well.

As a bonus, good planning can improve classroom management. Some teachers may not appear to plan, but although they don't have lots of paperwork, they are highly experienced and have internalised the process.

Activity 1.1 Anticipating problems

1   Read the beginning of the following imaginary scenario and the lesson plan.

Paul, a trainee teacher, has been asked to take over a Year 7, mixed ability, mixed gender class of twenty-three pupils for their ICT lessons. They are usually very well behaved. The class has had one hour a week of ICT for two months,

---

Activity 1.1 *continued*

and they have been creating a multimedia presentation about themselves. The next stage is for the pupils to demonstrate to the class what they have done and for them to receive feedback from their peers. The class teacher has told Paul to plan the remaining part of the unit as he sees fit. Some pupils had worked on the presentations at home. Paul has been teaching in the school for two weeks, but this is his first lesson with this class.

He has produced the rough plan shown in Figure 1.1.

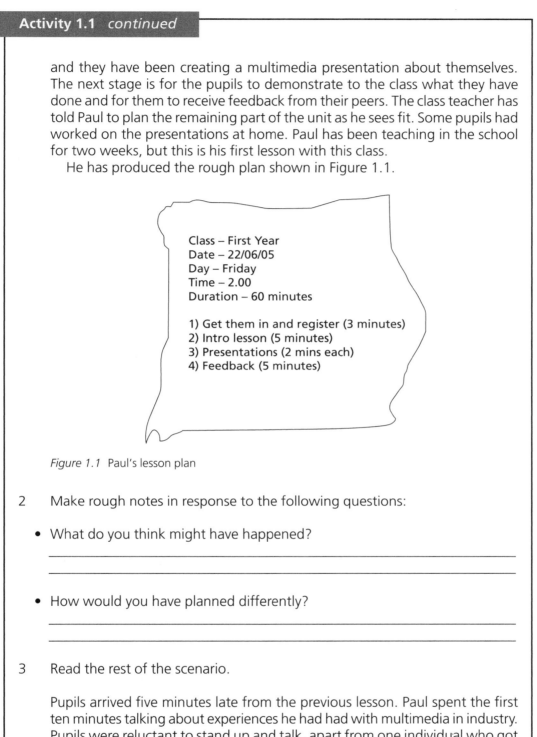

Class – First Year
Date – 22/06/05
Day – Friday
Time – 2.00
Duration – 60 minutes

1) Get them in and register (3 minutes)
2) Intro lesson (5 minutes)
3) Presentations (2 mins each)
4) Feedback (5 minutes)

Figure 1.1 Paul's lesson plan

2 Make rough notes in response to the following questions:

• What do you think might have happened?

  _____

  _____

• How would you have planned differently?

  _____

  _____

3 Read the rest of the scenario.

Pupils arrived five minutes late from the previous lesson. Paul spent the first ten minutes talking about experiences he had had with multimedia in industry. Pupils were reluctant to stand up and talk, apart from one individual who got up first and spent eight minutes talking largely about his favourite football team. The feedback from other pupils turned into an argument. One pupil broke down in tears when asked to stand up at the front. Some pupils found that features they had added to the presentation at home did not work in school. Five pupils did not have the work finished, as they had been on a school trip the previous week. The pupils had included sound, but the stand-alone laptop linked to the projector had insufficient volume for the class to

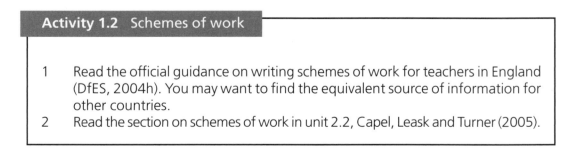

Activity 1.1 *continued*

hear. Some pupils brought work from home on external storage devices, which meant they needed extra time to load the file. Two pupils could not find their files on the network. Time ran out, with not all pupils presenting.

4 Make further notes in response to these questions:

• Which of Paul's problems did you anticipate?

_____

• How could each of these problems have been avoided?

_____
_____

The scenario in Activity 1.1 has been devised to highlight the need for careful planning. We do not expect your experience to be like this during your training, because of the support for the planning process that you will receive.

WHAT DO WE MEAN BY PLANNING?

To plan is to 'arrange a method or course of action thought out in advance' (*Oxford Paperback Dictionary*, 1994).

When beginning to teach you are most likely to focus on short-term planning, i.e. lesson planning. However, you must take account of longer-term plans, so that you know if you are teaching the right things at the right time.

Long-term teaching plan

A scheme of work might cover two years for an examination course or a single year of KS3. This would usually be written by a team or staff member under the direction of the head of department. You need to be familiar with the scheme of work in order to know whether you are on track or need to adapt your planning.

Activity 1.2 Schemes of work

1 Read the official guidance on writing schemes of work for teachers in England (DfES, 2004h). You may want to find the equivalent source of information for other countries.
2 Read the section on schemes of work in unit 2.2, Capel, Leask and Turner (2005).

Medium-term teaching plan

This is a plan for a topic that covers a number of weeks or a half term, i.e. a unit of work. You will need to write these for each class you teach. Starting with the scheme of work, you need to plan out how you will meet the required objectives in the time available. Be sure to check the school calendar and take account of such things as Bank Holidays, training days, assemblies or work experience that may use up your time, or forthcoming network maintenance that may force you to carry out non-computer-based ICT work.

An example of a medium-term ICT plan template and a completed example are given in Appendix A.

Short-term plan

This is an individual lesson plan and will be expected to contain aims and objectives.

Aims and objectives are often confused, though if you have done Activity 1.2 you should be clearer about the distinction. For our purposes we will adopt the following definitions, although they may be slightly different from those used on your course.

'Aims' should relate to the general skills, knowledge and understanding you want the pupils to attain, for instance: 'understanding the use of computers as a simulation tool' or 'ability to use spreadsheets to model cash flow'. The same aims may be applicable to more than one lesson.

Learning 'objectives' concern more specific knowledge or skills that you intend pupils to learn in order to reach the aim, for instance:

- ability to use formulas and absolute cell referencing;
- understanding why a spreadsheet is an appropriate tool for modelling cash flow.

All lessons must have objectives, by which you can measure success. Objectives are not the actual task, so that 'Complete Worksheet 3' is not an objective. We will use the term 'task outcomes' to represent the external product of pupils' learning activity, such as 'printout of spreadsheet showing formulas' or 'oral explanation of the role of a spreadsheet in modelling cash flow'. Always bear in mind that the purpose of the lesson is to achieve the learning objectives, not the task outcomes.

Note that commercially produced plans and government exemplars of long-term, medium-term and short-term plans are available, but bear in mind that they were produced in a different context. They are useful to look at, but need changing to take account of your pupils, your school and your circumstances. You must adapt them, or develop your own. It is important to know what is a statutory requirement, however. For instance, in England the KS3 strategy is not statutory, but the National Curriculum is. As long as you meet statutory requirements it is up to you and your school how this is achieved.

HOW TO START PLANNING AND PREPARING AN ICT LESSON

Here is a list of issues and advice to help you avoid common mistakes in planning and preparation of lessons:

- Be aware of the longer-term aims and requirements, and plan your lessons knowing where they fit the scheme of work and medium-term plan.
- Check that equipment works; for instance 'sound', as in Paul's lesson described earlier in the chapter.
- Check the compatibility of the software on the computers you are going to use; it may be a different version from the one you use at home.
- Work hard on understanding the resources in advance to avoid being exposed:

  - technically; for instance you need to be able to fix simple hardware problems such as a printer jam, putting paper in a printer, getting the whiteboard display working.
  - in terms of subject knowledge; you need to know and understand the software or theory you are going to use.

- pedagogically; make sure that you use teaching styles that are suitable for the pupils.

- Know the pupils' prior experience; avoid teaching the same thing too many times, but check what they remember from before.
- Do not overestimate/underestimate the pupils' abilities.
- Have good time management; for instance avoid running out of time to include key aspects of the lesson.
- Develop flexibility: adapt your plan/lesson to accommodate for the unexpected.
- Have a 'plan B' – and a 'plan C' – in case you have to abandon plan A.
- Include other adults who will be in the classroom; brief them clearly about what you want them to do.
- Plan transitions; for instance how and when pupils move, how you get them to save and log off.
- Consider possible health and safety issues; for instance, storage and location of bags, making sure projector leads are not where pupils will trip over them.
- If planning written work, have spare pens and pencils available. Pupils tend to think that because it is ICT they do not need to bring them.

Some of these points will be amplified in Chapter 2.

It is important to take the time to visualise what will happen if you follow the plan with that class. Visualisation is that technique athletes use to picture/rehearse what will occur, before they actually start. It is well worth running the whole lesson through in your mind to anticipate how it will go and what might go wrong. If need be, you can then adjust the plan and avoid the problem.

Activity 1.3 Your planning checklist

Add to the list of advice above to develop your own planning checklist to fit the circumstances in your school.

------------------------------------ ------------------------------------
------------------------------------ ------------------------------------
------------------------------------ ------------------------------------
------------------------------------ ------------------------------------

---

Before you plan, do your research on the pupils you are teaching. Talk to the class ICT teacher, other teachers of this class, form teachers, SEN (Special Educational Needs) coordinator, other adults working with the pupils, and, if appropriate, the pupils themselves. Find out the following – it will help you plan better:

- Class
- Age
- Ability range
- Names
- Seating plan
- Any pupils with special educational needs (SEN) – statemented or not
- Any pupils with Additional Educational Needs (AEN) – gifted and talented (in what?)
- Pupils with English as an additional language (EAL)
- Pupils with behavioural, emotional or social issues
- Others you need to know about

- Is there any data available on them?
- Are there targets for them?
- What is their prior learning?

It is important that you know who to consult and seek support from. If in doubt, ask for advice.

Consider in detail what they are to learn:

- Which scheme of work/syllabus should you be using?
- What point in the long-term/medium-term plan have the pupils reached?
- What have they done before (prior learning)?
- What is the progress for each pupil? They will not all be at the same point.
- What are they to learn next?
- What are the resources you have available?
- What are the deadlines for this topic/section/unit?
- How will you need to adapt the planning and resources for these pupils?

Now you can begin to plan lessons. When you do, there are key questions to ask about the plan to test its quality (see Table 1.1).

Many of these key questions can also be applied to medium- and long-term planning.

It is a long list, and your early plans may not address all these points. You may be given advice about the elements you need to focus on initially and then areas for development.

There are many examples of lesson plan formats (see Capel, Leask and Turner (2005) Unit 2.2, or Stephens and Crawley (2002) Chapter 3, for two such examples). Appendix A of this

Table 1.1 Key questions for lesson planning

- Has the plan got clear and appropriate aims/objectives that the pupils will understand?
- Does it clearly link activities to objectives?
- Does it show how the objectives will be assessed?
- If appropriate, does it show cross-curricular themes and links, i.e. literacy and numeracy?
- Does it encourage teaching and learning activities relevant to the actual pupils? Consider group, paired and individual work; ease of delivery; known and anticipated pupil errors and misconceptions; how to make difficult concepts understandable; using creative approaches.
- Does it take account of the learning styles of the pupils? For instance, you should try to provide for pupils with visual, auditory and kinaesthetic preferences, and consider other preferred learning styles (see Capel, Leask and Turner (2005), unit 5).
- Is it flexible?
- Does it identify appropriate resources? Are the ICT tools up-to-date and ready to use? Are you clear about the roles of other adults in the lesson?
- Will it be relevant, interesting, motivating and encourage creativity for pupils?
- Is the sequence of activities sensible?
- Does it have an appropriate balance between knowledge, skills and understanding? An ICT lesson should not be purely about skills.
- Does it link to life outside school?
- Does it promote independent learning? Your ultimate aim is to develop autonomous users of ICT.
- Does it take account of pupil prior learning (in ICT and other areas)?
- Does it differentiate appropriately across the range of abilities (in ICT and Key Skills) and include all pupils in that class?
- Are timings realistic, including transitions and time for plenaries?
- Is the assessment recordable? This is not relevant in every lesson but you do have to record assessment at some stage.
- Does it have all the relevant contextual information, including class, time, place? Does it identify pupils with particular needs including those with an IEP (Individual Education Plan), the more able and those with behavioural problems? Does it refer to the National Curriculum and/or longer-term plans?
- Have you got a back-up lesson prepared?
- Do you have the required subject and technical knowledge?

book has some templates and exemplars specific to ICT, produced by teachers, which have worked well for them.

A good lesson plan template should:

- be easy to use;
- be understandable to you;
- be understandable to others;
- have a suitable layout, e.g. not full of boxes of fixed size; sometimes a section will need more detail than at other times, so use an electronic table.

Having done the plan, ask someone else to look through it (class teacher, your mentor). They may notice things that you have not realised.

Activity 1.4 Advice for the trainee teacher

Having read all the above, what advice would you give to Paul, the trainee teacher, if you had observed the lesson in the scenario described earlier in the chapter? (The tutor's advice is given at the end of the chapter.)

_____

_____

_____

_____

PLANNING FOR COURSEWORK

You have to plan just as much for a good coursework lesson as for any other lesson and you need to monitor the pupils' progress and keep careful records. This can help avoid any panic as the coursework submission date approaches.

You may sometimes gain the impression that experienced teachers do not plan coursework lessons, and that the pupils 'just come in and get on with it'. Pupils can only 'get on with it' if they know what to get on with and how to do so, so whereas pupils may appear to you to be getting on with it with little direction, you will find that careful planning and communication with pupils has taken place before you became involved with the class. You must plan coursework lessons just as carefully as those where you are demonstrating and explaining new ideas, so that you are clear about expectations and can remind pupils about them.

Here is some advice concerning the planning of coursework activity:

- Start with a medium-term plan – what have they got to do and by when?
- Make sure you and they know the criteria used for assessing the coursework.
- Break the coursework down into suitable sections and set, share and use deadlines for each section. This is critical. If you do not set, share and keep to deadlines, pupils will get behind, and you will not know until it is too late.
- Work with the pupils to identify the skills, knowledge and understanding they need to have for each piece of work and plan to revise this if necessary.
- Each pupil should have and know their individual targets for each lesson, relating to their ability.
- Use a simple system for keeping records of progress and targets.

A common strategy used to support coursework planning is to display deadlines and time-lines clearly in the room and to send the dates to parents and senior managers.

An individual lesson may then consist of checking that pupils know their targets at the start of the lesson and possibly introducing a little theory or reinforcing a concept, setting them on task, monitoring their individual progress against their targets (helping or emphasising where necessary) and finishing by rechecking progress and sharing good practice with the whole class. Look at KS4 Example Lesson Plan in Appendix A.

Activity 1.5 Producing a lesson plan

1   Having read the chapter, produce a lesson plan for the lesson in the scenario described earlier in the chapter.
2   Apply the key questions in Table 1.1 to it. Could you improve it? How?
3   Look at your own current plan, look at the examples provided in Appendix A, and then produce a lesson plan template for yourself.

SUMMARY OF THE TUTOR'S ADVICE TO PAUL, THE TRAINEE TEACHER, FOLLOWING HIS OBSERVED LESSON

- Plan properly in short and medium term. There are three lessons remaining for this unit, so the work could and should take more than one lesson.
- Explain to pupils clearly what is expected of them, and perhaps show them an example of how a slide presentation is used to support a talk about a topic.
- Take account of the time of day and be sensitive to your pupils.
- Be realistic with time, and bear in mind that transitions between presentations are not fast.
- Check that equipment works properly.
- Check software compatibility between home and school and have a strategy for dealing with this.
- Be flexible. The lesson started late, so you needed to adapt the plan.
- Be positive and supportive with pupils, as presentations may be stressful for them.
- Give guidelines to pupils on how to evaluate and give feedback before you start.
- You should have known that pupils were absent and taken account of this.

FURTHER READING

Brooks, V., Abbott, I. and Bills, L. (eds) (2004) *Preparing to Teach in Secondary Schools*, Maidenhead: Open University Press. Chapter 5, Planning for learning.

Capel, S., Leask, M. and Turner, T. (eds) (2005) *Learning to Teach in the Secondary School*, 3rd edn, London: RoutledgeFalmer. Unit 2.2, Schemes of work and lesson planning.

Cowley, S. (2003) *Getting the Buggers to Behave 2*, London: Continuum. Chapter 6, Planning for behaviour management.

Kyriacou, C. (2001) *Essential Teaching Skills*, 2nd edn, Cheltenham: Nelson Thornes. Chapter 2, Planning and preparation.

Stephens, P. and Crawley, T. (2002) *Becoming an Effective Teacher*, Cheltenham: Nelson Thornes. Chapter 3, Teaching your subject.

WEBSITES

Lesson planning:
www.teachernet.gov.uk/teachinginengland/detail.cfm?id=216

Curriculum planning:
www.teachernet.gov.uk/teachinginengland/detail.cfm?id=553

Planning checklist:
www.teachernet.gov.uk/teachinginengland/download/documents/Planning%20checklist.doc

Behaviour management:
www.teachernet.gov.uk/teachinginengland/detail.cfm?id=538.

Chapter 2 Classroom interaction

GEOFF WHITE AND ANDREW CONNELL

INTRODUCTION

In this chapter we look at factors affecting the success of teaching and learning, which if not given due attention can mean that your plans will be ineffective in practice. These factors include pupils' welfare, the physical environment, classroom layout, the layout of computer systems, the working patterns in the classroom, resource organisation, the roles of other adults in the classroom such as learning support assistants, and other organisational factors.

By the end of this chapter you should:

- understand how these factors have an impact on the quality of teaching and learning.

ACTIVITIES IN THE ICT CLASSROOM

In a typical ICT lesson you may see some of the following:

- The teacher introducing a new topic whilst standing at the front of the class.
- Pupils watch a demonstration via a digital projector.
- The teacher explains the task that pupils are to carry out.
- Pupils disperse to use computers for the task.
- The teacher circulates among the class members offering help whenever it is needed.
- The teacher conducts a plenary session to review what pupils have learned from the work.

Activity 2.1 A typical ICT lesson

Make a list of other things the teacher may do during the lesson.

_____   _____
_____   _____
_____   _____
_____   _____

Here are some possibilities that you may observe. The teacher may:

- answer questions from members of the class;
- ask the class as a whole a series of questions;
- ask a pupil to show something to the class;
- split the class into groups to discuss an issue or complete a task together;
- make suggestions for improvements either to the class as a whole or to individuals;
- call the class together to explain something which has concerned a number of individuals;
- demonstrate something by taking over control of everyone's computers;
- talk to individuals about pastoral matters.

More detail concerning many of these and other strategies can be found in Kennewell *et al.* (2003), particularly Chapters 5 and 6.

During a good lesson, the teacher engages in a range of activities with the pupils. The quality of these interactions can be influenced by a wide range of factors that you must consider.

WELFARE FACTORS AND THE PHYSICAL ENVIRONMENT

It is important to consider the welfare of those in the classroom in order to optimise motivation – for you and the pupils. This means considering a variety of factors.

Motivation

The motivation of your pupils is very important if they are to do well. Child (1997) describes motivation as being of two kinds, intrinsic and extrinsic. Intrinsic motivation stems from a sense of achievement at having solved a difficult problem, perhaps developing a model based on a spreadsheet, while extrinsic motivation stems from external considerations, e.g. praise from the teacher or the need to complete some coursework by a given deadline.

However, before pupils can become motivated they must have been provided with what Maslow (1970) describes as lower-level needs. At the very basic level, these are listed as physiological needs, e.g. food and warmth, and then physical needs such as a safe and comfortable working environment. Maslow suggests that, without these, pupils will not reach the higher levels of his motivational hierarchy.

This means that before your pupils can work effectively you must do your best to provide them with a comfortable and safe environment.

Health and safety issues

The school has a corporate responsibility for the health and safety of all people in the school. As a teacher you must be aware of the school's Health and Safety Policy and who to report problems to. There are additional issues for the ICT classroom as it is potentially a hazardous place, full of electrical equipment.

Typical hazards to look out for will include trailing electrical wires and network cables, loose connections on computers and peripherals, faulty power points and electrical plugs.

Use of resources appropriately

With the increasing use of the internet in education most schools will have devised an internet policy. As a minimum, schools will include a ban on accessing unsuitable sites for children, including those of a pornographic, violent, or racist nature. However there will be many other kinds of site which the school may deem to be unsuitable.

The use of the internet has a close bearing on the use of the school's network in general and so the policy is likely to include guidelines and rules on the use of those systems too. Having devised their policy, the school may well require both parents and pupils to sign a form in which they agree to abide by the policy. Passwords might not be issued until this has been done, and network access might be suspended for any breach.

The school and ICT department should also have policies and promote good practice on such things as the use of games, the loan of software and copyright issues. You must know these policies and follow them.

Displays

An ICT classroom can be made to look particularly attractive and, most importantly, you can support learning with the imaginative use of wall displays. Use of displays is often a priority in primary classrooms but as Lang (2004: 303) observes, 'display in classrooms is often a weak area in secondary schools'. It is essential to regularly update the material which is shown, to keep it current and tidy.

Many companies provide suitable and free posters which, whilst drawing attention to their products, also include an educational element. Examples include posters on network topographies, input and output devices, and so on. Posters tend to be technical in nature, but can support a topic or keywords.

Display of keywords enables pupils to see important specialist vocabulary much more frequently that they would in the normal course of activity, and the displays can be used as prompts when questioning pupils. The Secondary National Strategy for England gives lists of keywords for each topic area. For example, Year 7, Unit 5, Lesson 1 (DfES, 2002) covers the interrogation of a database. The keywords given for this lesson include 'database', 'field' and 'numeric data'. It would be useful to display the keyword list while this lesson takes place and then add to the display as the class progresses through the six lessons that comprise this unit.

Examples of pupils' work can be displayed on the wall. This can be used to provide ideas and models of good practice, and in any case most pupils like to feel that their work is valued. It is not essential that every piece is perfect every time, as this could exclude some pupils. However, its quality should be high, at least in terms of its appearance and accuracy.

A particularly useful strategy is to display exemplar work, to show pupils your expectations. However, it is essential to annotate the work to show them why the work is 'good' or worth a particular mark/grade. For example, you might display GCSE coursework to illustrate a grade A, a grade C and a grade D. These should clearly show, through annotation, why the grades are different.

Weather and room temperature

You should be aware of the temperature in the room. This is very important in an ICT room as monitors in particular generate a lot of heat and the room can warm up to an unacceptable level if they are left on all the time. Try to have periods during the lesson when monitors can be switched off. You can have a routine whereby pupils turn off their monitors when you wish to talk to them as a group. Consider opening windows. If you have air conditioning, use this but be aware that it might generate background noise. You also want to avoid a room being too cold, as pupils will not be able to concentrate on the learning.

The weather outside can be a factor in your lessons. For example, if it is windy, pupils are often difficult to settle. If it is very sunny, they can get lethargic. If it snows during a lesson, they may rush to the windows and then ask if the school will close. If it is very wet they may arrive in the room with wet clothes, which is a potential health and safety issue. If they have been kept in at break, they may be restless. If you are aware of potential issues due to weather, you can then respond accordingly.

Interruptions

A factor which is particularly significant for ICT is that lessons can be subject to regular disturbances, which you will have to deal with. For example, other teachers send pupils to your classroom to ask if they can use a spare machine; staff may want to use a machine; if you have the network printer in your room people come to collect printouts; if staff or pupils nearby have a problem with ICT they interrupt to ask for help; if the head is showing people round the school, they bring them in to show them the 'state of the art' ICT facilities. As a new teacher this can be very distracting, but you will get used to it. The pupils seem to accept it quite readily.

Noise can be another factor. External noise, such as a building project, may mean having to keep windows shut, even if it is warm. Fans in the computers and air conditioning can generate a constant background noise that you have to cope with.

Other welfare factors

Be aware that if you are 'under the weather', you might not perform to your best and you may be less tolerant than usual. Likewise, be aware that pupils may be ill too, and may not perform as well as usual.

Computers produce ozone, and this can build up in a computer room. It can affect some people, so try to ventilate the room regularly. Having some plants in the room can help.

Your voice is an essential tool and can be under a lot of strain. Protect it by 'projecting' rather than shouting. Drink water and avoid too much caffeine or alcohol.

Activity 2.2 Environmental and welfare factors

Make a list of the other environmental or welfare factors that might impact on the learning in your classroom. Using the above and your list, discuss the factors and place them in order of the level of impact on learning in your classroom. Think in particular about those children with less than perfect hearing and vision.

_____

_____

_____

CLASSROOM LAYOUTS

The layout of the classroom affects the style of the teaching. In the traditional classroom, as shown in the recent picture of a classroom in China (Figure 2.1), the teacher is likely to adopt a 'teacher-centered' approach, instructing the class, telling them about the subject and expecting the class to copy notes from the blackboard or books.

In the modern classroom with total access to ICT (Figure 2.2), our expectations of the approach to teaching and learning are different.

Figure 2.1 Traditional classroom

Figure 2.2 Digital classroom

Activity 2.3   Different layouts

Compare the scene in Figure 2.1 with Figure 2.2 and list the differences. What has stayed the same?

_____

_____

Figure 2.3 shows another modern layout. How does this compare with the classrooms of Figures 2.1 and 2.2?

Figure 2.3 Learning styles classroom (see Prashnig, 2006)

COMPUTER ROOM LAYOUT

There are a number of possible layouts for the computers in the ICT room. Common ones include the following:

- around the edge of the room, against the walls;
- across the room in rows;
- islands.

Activity 2.4   Computer room layouts

What are the strengths and weakness of the three common layouts above?

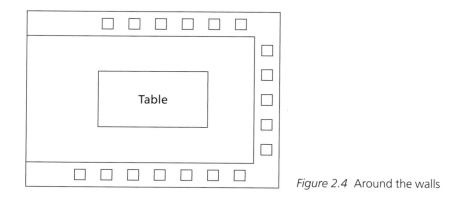

Figure 2.4 Around the walls

Figure 2.4 shows what is probably the most common layout encountered in our schools. It has the advantage that the teacher can see exactly what every pupil is doing as they can see all the screens from anywhere in the room. Also, if the room is large enough, tables in the centre of the room can accommodate a whole class for non-computer work.

The disadvantages are:

- There will always be some pupils whose backs are turned towards the teacher. This makes whole class teaching difficult.
- The layout is wasteful in terms of space. In a small room, there may not be room for a class set of computers and there may be insufficient tables for all pupils to sit away from the computers.

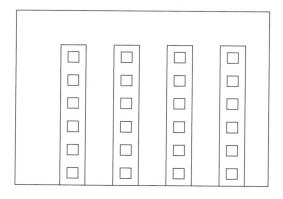

Figure 2.5 In rows

The advantage of the layout in figure 2.5 is that all the pupils are facing towards the front of the class. This is ideal when the teacher needs to address the whole class. Note that this classroom is equipped with a projector mounted on the ceiling and everyone can see the screen without having to move.

The disadvantages are:

- The teacher cannot see what everyone is doing unless he positions himself at the back of the room, clearly a difficulty if teaching is carried out from the front.
- If the rows are too close it may be difficult for the teacher to circulate. Note that, in this classroom, there is plenty of space between the rows.
- There may be no space for pupils to carry out non-computer work.

Figure 2.6 shows a popular configuration in that it makes good use of the available space, and the teacher can circulate easily.

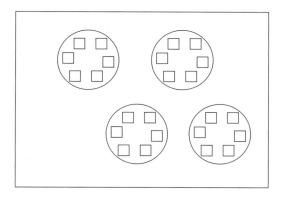

Figure 2.6 As islands

The drawback is that, as in the case of having the computers around the edge of the room, some pupils will have their backs to the teacher. Note that this classroom has sufficient room to have some computers around the edge as well and some space between the computers for other activities.

WORKING PATTERNS

Once it was the norm that pupils would have to share computers, but this was out of necessity rather than choice. Schools are far better equipped with ICT equipment now, but the teacher will often suggest that pupils work in pairs anyway, for reasons concerned with effective learning.

Activity 2.5 Single and paired working

Make a list of some advantages and disadvantages of single and paired working. Focus particularly on advantages in terms of pupil learning.

_____

_____

_____

_____

Individual work

It is only by requiring pupils to work on their own that you can be really sure about their capabilities. Furthermore, it provides some practice for test conditions.

At the time of writing, schools in England are piloting an onscreen Key Stage 3 test which would normally be taken at the end of Year 9. This test presents candidates with a scenario, such as the writing of an article for a local newspaper. The candidate receives initial suggestions from their editor as to where they might look for relevant information. If the candidate responds to this and makes clear progress they will be scored appropriately by the system.

Should the candidate be unsure as to how to proceed they will be prompted by the system, but this will result in a lower score. Despite the innovative nature of this test the candidate is still required to work alone. This is also true of the various practical examinations set by examination boards.

Projects and practical assignments required for GCSE schemes are undertaken in a normal classroom environment and it is unrealistic to expect that they will be carried out under examination conditions. However, candidates must confirm that the work they have done is their own and that there has been no collaboration.

In the case of GCSE Applied, the rules are more stringent. The externally assessed units are practical in nature but must be carried out under examination conditions. This means that pupils are not allowed to talk to each other. The tasks require pupils to carry out research which they are allowed to do prior to the examination. However, they are only allowed to take their own notes into the examination sessions and must not have access to the internet.

Working in pairs

There are benefits to working in pairs for certain learning activities: pupils are able to help each other and can 'bounce' ideas off each other. Pupils also have an opportunity to develop their social skills.

However, the teacher must be careful. How should the pupils be paired up? Left to their own devices they will probably choose to work with their friends, but this may not be the best choice. It is important that the teacher knows the pupils well, so that the best pairings are chosen for a particular task. Whatever system of pairing is used, the teacher will have to be vigilant in order to ensure that real progress is made by everyone.

If pupils are paired such that one is more able than the other, there is an expectation that the more able should help the less able. The less able pupil may feel perfectly happy with this as there is a kind of informal arrangement between friends but there is the danger that the more able pupil will do all the work and the other member of the pair will just watch. Handled well, however, the arrangement can benefit the more able pupil too, helping them develop understanding through explaining to the other pupil.

You might feel that pupils should be paired so that each member is of the same level of ability. This may be satisfactory in the case of more able pupils, but a pair of less able pupils may find themselves struggling with the work.

The teacher will also need to devise a system which ensures that individuals can be assessed. There will be little useful evidence gained if, for instance, a high grade is awarded for a piece of work to two pupils when only one of them has actually done it.

Working in groups

This has the benefit of greater socialisation and of preparing the pupils for teamwork, a skill needed in the 'real world'. It also allows scarce resources to be shared. However, as with paired work, selection of group members must be done carefully by the teacher. It may be helpful to assign a specific role to each pupil in the group, in order to match the work to their potential for learning and ensure that all can contribute.

These issues are discussed further in Kennewell *et al.* (2003), Chapters 6 and 7.

RESOURCE ORGANISATION

You may have access to many resources in the school, or you may create material yourself. Whatever resources you have, it is important to organise them effectively in order to maximise pupils' learning opportunities.

Activity 2.6 Organising your resources

If your resources are not well organised, what are the potential barriers to learning? Make a list. If possible, discuss this with colleagues.

_____

_____

Here is a list of possible things you may have considered.

- Username and password. You must know the system for allocating usernames and passwords in your school, but be cautious about trying to deal with forgotten passwords yourself because you can waste a great deal of time from your lesson.
- Printed resources, such as handouts, worksheets and textbooks. Make sure you have enough copies, but printed resources are expensive and you should consider whether electronic resources in a shared area might be better.
- Pupil absence. Have a strategy for dealing with pupil absence, for example a folder containing any resources they may have missed.
- Software. Make sure you have the correct software in the room, that it works and that it is the version you require (if not, you will have to adapt).
- Projection devices (e.g. OHP, interactive whiteboard, LCD projector). Be familiar with how to use them, know where pens, remote controls or other relevant equipment are stored. Have a back-up plan in case it fails.
- Network failure. Have contingency plans in case of complete failure of your hardware or some other major disruption (see Chapter 1).
- Handing out and collecting in. Have a strategy for organised handing out of books, worksheets, equipment, etc. and another for collecting things in. Have a strategy for collection and distribution of printouts.
- Printers and other peripheral devices. Make sure they work properly and that pupils use them in an appropriate way, e.g. pupils should not all print at the same time.
- Computers. Check you have enough working computers for the group size. Plan carefully if you have to change your approach.
- Keys. ICT rooms are often kept locked, so you need a key or a way to gain access.

Activity 2.7   Levels of impact

Discuss the above list and any potential problems you have thought of. Place the various points in order of the level of impact each may have on the learning in a lesson.

OTHER ORGANISATIONAL FACTORS

Other adults in the classroom

You will often find yourself in charge of a classroom in which other adults are present: as well as the normal teacher, there may be learning support assistants or a technician. It is important to be clear about their roles in managing learning and behaviour for particular pupils and the whole class. You should try to ascertain their potential for helping pupils, in terms of their ICT skills and ability to explain ideas. It is wise to be clear in advance about who is responsible for class organisation and disciplinary decisions, in order to maintain a positive and consistent approach to class management.

System maintenance procedures

Do you know the correct procedures for the reporting and fixing of hardware and software problems? Do you use them correctly? How long will it take for a broken computer to be fixed? This may have an impact on a number of your lessons.

Retaining attention for a plenary review

You should normally end a lesson with a review of the activity and learning, which involves the whole class together. However, if you first tell pupils to save and log off (do remind them to save!), they may switch their attention off too. Your carefully planned review then becomes hard work. One possible approach is to:

- Tell them to stop working 10 or 15 minutes from the end of the lesson – 'switch monitors off and face me, but do not pack up'.
- Carry out the review activity.
- Let them back on the computers for a few minutes.
- Now when you say 'save and log off' it is close to the end of the lesson. Pupils finish more quickly and you have less stress.

Other ideas are discussed in Chapter 10.

New technologies

At the time of writing, a number of new technologies are becoming widespread in classrooms, including interactive whiteboards, videoconferencing, electronic voting systems, and monitoring systems. Further technologies will emerge in due course (see also Part 3 of this book). It is clear that they offer important new opportunities to help teachers manage their resources, engage learners and support tasks which can stimulate new ways of learning. However, the pedagogy associated with new technologies is still being developed. As they arrive in schools you will need to become familiar with their use, be involved in the debates that ensue and think carefully about how you will plan and organise to enhance learning.

SUMMARY

One of the key factors in successful lessons is your attention to the classroom environment. This chapter has highlighted a variety of issues which you will need to take into account when planning and preparing lessons. You will not be able to control all the factors involved, but your increasing awareness of their influence will enable you better to adapt your teaching to the particular setting in which you are working.

FURTHER READING

DfES (2004c) *Key Stage 3 National Strategy, Pedagogy and practice Unit 20: Classroom management*, London: DfES. Available at http://www.standards.dfes.gov.uk/keystage3/respub/sec_pptl0, accessed 9 June 2005.

WEBSITES

Becta Schools support website (particularly under the headings 'Learning and Teaching' and 'Technology') http://schools.becta.org.uk/.

Chapter 3   **Effective assessment**

NEIL STANLEY AND PHIL DUGGAN

INTRODUCTION

In this chapter we will consider what we mean by assessment and the different types of assessment techniques. We will highlight the need to plan lesson objectives and outcomes that can be assessed, identify the common mistakes made in assessment and consider the role of 'Assessment for Learning' in raising attainment. We will explain what moderation is and why it is necessary, and finally look at practical strategies to help you collect evidence and judge pupil progress.

Teaching is like a house of cards with complex interlinking steps between elements. As we discussed in Chapter 1, planning is fundamental to success, and successful planning needs a clear knowledge of what knowledge, skills and understanding your learners have. The concept of assessment and the ability to use various strategies appropriately are key to achieving this.

This chapter focuses on good practice in the management of the monitoring and recording aspects of the assessment process. Assessment needs to be a holistic process, founded in planning, and developing from and for the needs of the learners.

By this end of this chapter you should be able to:

- recognise and develop good assessment practice;
- share assessment criteria with pupils;
- give effective written and verbal feedback to pupils;
- conduct an effective moderation.

ASSESSMENT

Without assessment we do not know what our learners already know, when they have learnt something, what their rate of progress is and how we can best help them. Assessment is fundamental to planning, not an afterthought. Alongside this we need strategies for monitoring and recording this progress. Many, if not all, of these strategies should be shared with the learners so that they may develop their own skills in self-assessment and empower their own learning.

Teaching is a complex skill, requiring the teacher to juggle many issues. As a trainee you probably started with the planning issue and rapidly added the class management issue. Now you are trying to add in the monitoring and recording issue. No doubt you are feeling overwhelmed.

What is assessment?

Assessment *of* learning is a summative assessment to ascertain the level a child has reached which could be termly, annually or at the end of a key stage.

Assessment *for* learning is the ongoing day-to-day formative assessment that takes place to gather information on what a child or group of children understand or do not understand and how future teaching will be adapted to account for this. Effective ongoing day-to-day assessments would include effective questioning; observations of children during teaching and while they are working; holding discussions with children; analysing work and reporting to children; conducting tests and giving quick feedback and engaging children in the assessment process.

(DfES, 2005a)

Assessment types

Assessment types are well described elsewhere (Capel *et al.*, 2005; Kennewell *et al.*, 2003; Birmingham Grid for Learning, 2005) but Table 3.1 provides a brief summary.

Table 3.1 Types of assessment

Formal	A planned activity resulting in the award of a grade, level or mark. This should be designed to establish the extent to which learning objectives have been achieved. Results are recorded and shared with pupils.
Informal	Teachers regularly check the progress that pupils are making. It will often be a qualitative judgement, shared orally, following observation and/or questioning.
Summative	Provides information/evidence of what a pupil knows, understands and can do. Normally the final review of learning at the end of a learner's programme of study This usually results in the award of a grade, level or mark.
Baseline	A fact-finding process to gather evidence of a learner's abilities, experience and learning so far.
Formative	Provides information/evidence that will be helpful in determining how learning can be taken forward. Formative assessment must be used to inform future planning and may result in an interim grade, level or mark. It needs to involve the pupil in making judgements about attainment, progress and targets for improvement. This ought to be a continuous process of review throughout a programme to build up a profile of the individual learner, and to monitor and review and support their progress against targets.
Diagnostic	Pupils and teachers make structured judgements about achievement against clear criteria (learning objectives) highlighting gaps in skills, knowledge and understanding and should lead to strategies for closing these gaps and identifying any additional support needs.
Ipsative	A target-setting model where the learner is expected to make a particular amount of progress from an initially determined starting point based on their current personal abilities.
Peer	Pupils monitor each other's progress against known criteria and can report to individual pupils.
Self	Pupils monitor their own progress against known criteria or discussion with teachers and others. Learning objectives can be shared with pupils, who record evidence of progress as the work progresses.

Complete Table 3.2 by adding ticks to the relevant boxes to identify who would carry out that particular type of assessment. There may be more than one tick per assessment type.

Table 3.2 Assessment types

		This assessment can be used by:		
Assessment type	Example	The teacher	The learner	External body
Formal	Set examinations			
Informal	Observation used to suggest improvement			
Summative	Externally set examination			
Baseline	SAT results			
Formative	Project progress sheet and annotation			
Diagnostic	Specifically designed test			
Ipsative	'I want you to include an extra picture next time'			
Peer-	Group review of an individual's website			
Self-	Self-review checklist			

Frequently, summative marks are used to inform the next stage of learning and, if produced in the correct format, can be used in a formative manner. For assessment to be effective, the learner must be able to use the assessment information to improve their own learning and take ownership of how they can proceed. This is the real reason that assessment must be planned into the whole scheme of activity and must be designed so that, besides giving an indication of current skills and knowledge, it highlights how work might be improved.

Activity 3.2 Assessment events in a lesson

1 Observe a lesson and note the assessment events (or possible events) that occur. Talk to the teacher after the lesson about why they chose to do what they did in terms of assessment.
2 Consider a lesson that you have taught recently and try to identify the forms of assessment that you used in that lesson. (Note: you will be asked to revisit your response to this at the end of the section.)

_____
_____
_____

THE NEED TO PLAN ASSESSMENT

> . . . thinking through both the learning objectives and the expected learning outcomes in advance of the lesson is the key to successful lesson planning. The nature of the objectives will determine what teaching approach (or model) you use, and the strategies and techniques you will employ to ensure that the learning is effective and efficient.
>
> (DfES, 2004c:5)

Opportunities for assessment need to be identified at a very early stage when planning a lesson or a unit of work (see Chapter 1). The learning objectives specify the learning that is to take place in the lesson, while the task outcomes indicate the evidence that pupils must produce to indicate that the learning objectives have been met. This evidence can take a variety of different forms, from 'hard' evidence such as printouts and worksheets to 'soft' evidence such as question and answer, demonstrations and observations. Opportunities for pupils to generate evidence for assessment should be planned at a very early stage, but it should be noted that opportunities for assessment which have not been planned for will also frequently arise, and should be exploited.

The tools for measuring the outcomes of learning need to be shared with the learners, in a form that they can understand. These can range from the extremely complex (for example, the mark scheme associated with A2 level ICT project work put into appropriate language for students) to the more simple (for example, the 'I have' sheets in Figure 3.1 which some schools in England use with the Secondary National Strategy materials).

The Flickbook Project **Name:** ______________________

I have:

		Date	Tutor
Watched the Animation Process Video	☐	________	
Loaded Complete Animator	☐	________	
Created a simple animation of at least 5 frames	☐	________	____
Used 'inbetweening'	☐	________	
Saved my animation (name: ________)	☐	________	
Added a background	☐	________	____
Printed out my animation	☐	________	____
Storyboarded my main flickbook	☐	________	____
Created my main flickbook animation	☐	________	
Used the laminator	☐	________	
Made up my flickbook	☐	________	____
Incorporated a scanned graphic	☐	________	

I am happy about my final flickbook because:

I could improve my final flickbook if I:

Figure 3.1 An example of a simple 'I have' sheet

This sharing of information about assessment highlights the need for an introduction to lessons and for time at the end of a lesson to review the key expected learning (see Chapter 2).

With work based on existing schemes it will often still be necessary to go back, and identify and clarify the ideas that are to be covered in a unit and to re-map these on to teaching sessions. Remember it is the ideas (concepts, knowledge and skills) that you wish to cover that determine how and what you teach, not just a good idea for an activity (see Chapter 1).

It is also important to not let the assessment-evidence generation take over the learning activity in the classroom. Designing a major activity that builds up over time and that can address several outcomes will often be preferable to lots of small activities. However, as process is important, you will need to carefully design means for the learner tracking and presenting evidence of success. This may mean that you need to support the development of some sort of portfolio of evidence, and many younger and less able learners will need support in developing the skills needed to identify what should be included and how it might be annotated.

One way of approaching this, certainly with lower attaining secondary school learners, might be to use learning diaries or logs. These are writing frames that have been specifically designed to be used every now and then, when appropriate, to record progress. A writing frame is a document (paper or electronic) that provides a clear framework to which the learner can add text. For example, part way through a lesson when you hope to have covered some specific points, you may give a short series of questions to respond to. This may include a list of useful words, sentences to complete, or even paragraphs with key words to be added. You will find some examples for the Secondary National Strategy for England on the Lewisham LEA website (see Websites at the end of this chapter). Specific examples can be seen in Figure 3.2.

A database is a _____ collection of_____
[fields, structured, random, records]

Lesson 2: **During this lesson you will be learning to add images to your presentation to help get your message across.**		
Useful vocabulary Clip art, copyright, audience, fitness for purpose, images, appropriate, crop, manipulate, camera, scanner, blurred, detail	Q1 Where did you get some of your pictures from to insert in your presentation?	1. I inserted the pictures from c.. pa..
	Q2 What happens to a bitmap image (photograph) when it is enlarged?	2. When it enlarged a bitmap image becomes b.....d and loses its d....l
	Q3 What could you use to get images for your presentation?	
	Q4 What must you think about when choosing images for your presentation?	

Figure 3.2 Examples of writing frame elements

You may also need to plan the taking of 'snapshots' of work in progress, but constantly printing out large amounts of paper is a problem for the planet, for department budgets, and for your time. Electronic portfolios to store such work are beginning to appear, and you may wish to consider these.

MANAGEABLE ASSESSMENT

Assessment becomes manageable when it is focused, appropriate and targeted (remember the acronym FAT). Within a sequence of lessons, opportunities for informal and formative assessment should be built into the lesson planning. Peer- and self-assessment should

Activity 3.3 Learning diaries

Look at the Lewisham website (see Websites, p. 36) and study carefully any of the learning diaries you can download from there. Now consider a lesson you are about to teach and design a learning diary page that you might use in a plenary to help the learners understand what they have been expected to learn that day. Try it out. Remember we are all resistant to change, and as this may be different from their normal expected practice, your learners may be reluctant to participate at first. It is worth persevering in order to involve learners in their assessment.

take place on an ongoing basis, with diagnostic assessment occurring at regular intervals to inform progress and identify needs. Examples of simple peer- and self-assessment tools are given in Appendix B. By involving pupils in their assessment the whole process becomes more meaningful to them and definitely more manageable for you. The nature of assessment changes from something you do 'to' the pupils to something you do 'with' them.

It is important not to fall into the trap of thinking that every child has to be assessed in every single lesson. Careful consideration of what is being assessed, together with an understanding of why it is being assessed at that time, enables the strategic deployment of appropriate assessment techniques. There will be times when it is appropriate to assess the whole class, and other times when it is more useful to concentrate on smaller groups of pupils for the purposes of target setting.

RECORD KEEPING

Given the variety of evidence that can be used to form judgements of pupils' progress, accurate recording is essential. Many different types of recording techniques can be used to record evidence, ranging from formal mark books to collected data on summative assessment, to tick boxes and 'traffic light' systems for diagnostic assessment. For example, whilst doing practical work pupils may have access to a set of three coloured cards, red, amber and green. If they are managing well they show the green card, if they are absolutely unable to make progress they show the red and if they are working but could do with some help they show the amber. This system can be set up as flags located on top of the monitor. This system can also be used to collect feedback at the end of the lesson with the 'traffic lights' being included in a lesson review sheet or the learning diary.

Of particular importance is the need to record soft evidence (that is evidence that you may have obtained through informal observation or chance conversation). Videoing (with permission) pupils in the class can work well, but is often time-consuming and inconvenient. Often, having a well-set-up mark book that enables the teacher to note when a pupil has answered a question, demonstrated a skill or verbalised a concept is sufficient for the majority of assessment purposes. It is also vital that the mark book is set up in such a way as to enable the teacher to record pupil targets. Examples of such a mark book format are given in Figure 3.3.

Whatever assessment method is used, it is important to remember that during moderation (see later in this chapter) or levelling exercises, sufficient evidence should have been recorded so that other teachers looking at the same evidence would make the same judgement as to pupil attainment. To this end, it is good practice for a 'context' document to be produced setting the background of the assessment task, overviewing the soft evidence and explaining the thinking behind the judgements made. It is not necessary for a context document to be produced for every piece of work by every pupil, but it is useful for a document to be produced for those samples of work selected for examination by other teachers.

It is worth spending time designing a mark book or record book that suits your style of working and makes life easier for you. Although using a computer to hold the records may be desirable, it may not be the best mode for ease of use during lessons.

Activity 3.4   Effective assessment

A typical lesson plan for a trainee includes these learning objectives:

Pupils will be able to:

- *create records in a pre-designed table;*
- *understand the idea of a relationship between tables;*
- *create an appropriate link between two tables.*

These might be the task outcomes, indicating differentiated expectations:

- *Most pupils will enter a minimum of 15 records into their Customer table.*
- *Some pupils will enter a minimum of 3 records into their Product table.*
- *Most pupils will print out their data.*
- *Most pupils will link their tables.*

How would you effectively assess whether the learning objectives had been met?

MAKING JUDGEMENTS

It is important to remember when assessing that you are considering the quality of the work produced and the thinking behind it, not the quantity. Assessment should be integral to the whole year and not left until the end. You must provide regular opportunities for pupils to demonstrate higher levels of intellectual endeavour. In England and Wales, level criteria at age 14 are defined by the National Curriculum, but even if this were not the case it would be important to set out a way of identifying progression against expectations for the learners.

NC levels

As all pupils are expected to be given a level at the end of KS3, it is an important teacher skill to be able to judge the level of pupils' work. Many local authorities provide training to help to develop this skill and to provide opportunities for moderating a portfolio of work across several schools. It does need to be a portfolio of work because covering the range of the NC for ICT will require a broad collection of evidence.

Activity 3.5   KS3 portfolio of evidence

From your experiences, note down the typical contents of a portfolio of evidence for levelling at KS3 that you have observed being used.

_____

_____

Pupils' names are listed here

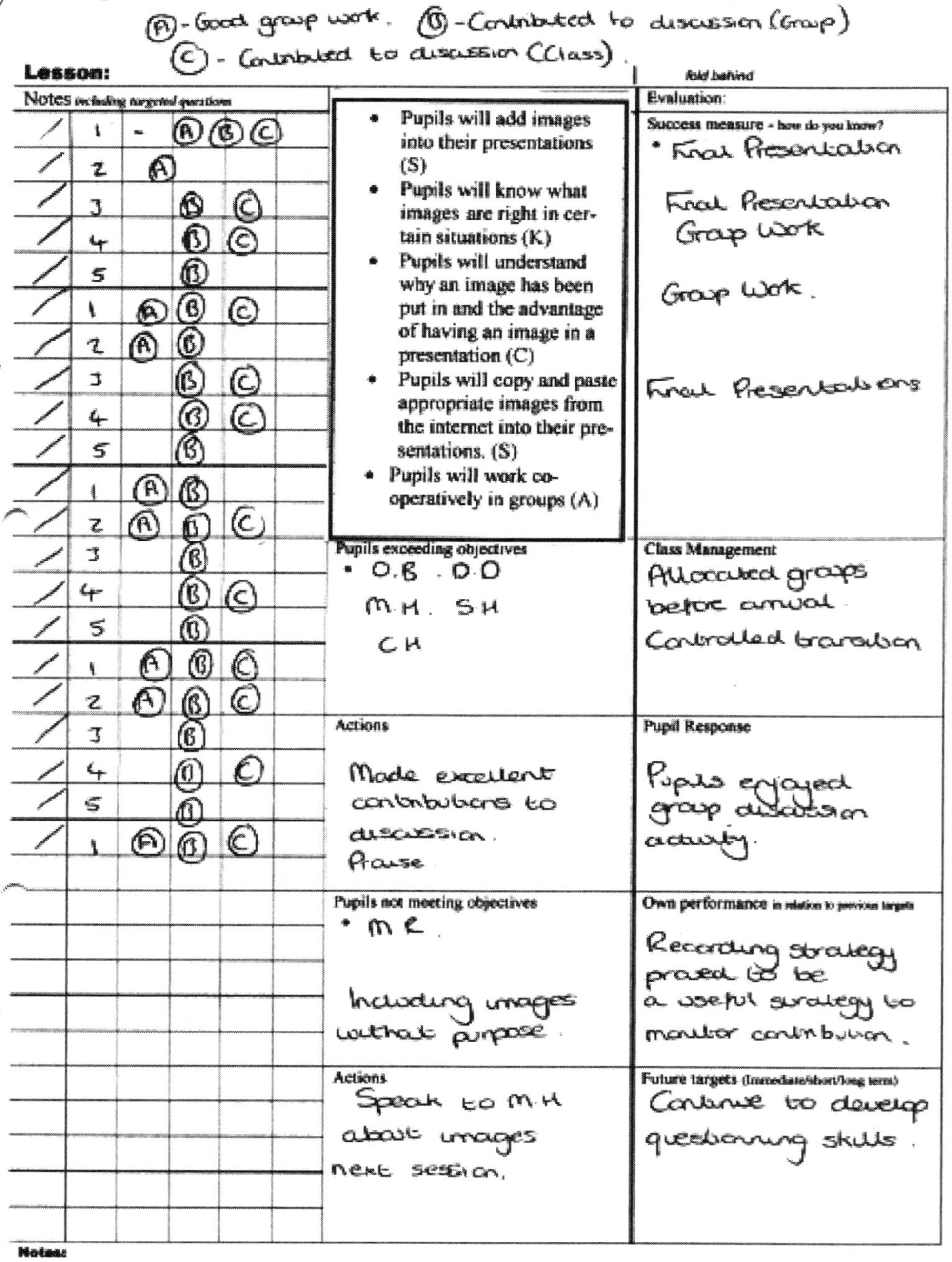

(A) - Good group work.   (B) - Contributed to discussion (Group)
(C) - Contributed to discussion (Class).

Lesson:

fold behind

Notes *including targeted questions*				Objectives	Evaluation:

Notes including targeted questions

/	1	—	(A) (B) (C)	
/	2	(A)		
/	3	(B) (C)		
/	4	(B) (C)		
/	5	(B)		
/	1	(A) (B) (C)		
/	2	(A) (B)		
/	3	(B) (C)		
/	4	(B) (C)		
/	5	(B)		
/	1	(A) (B)		
/	2	(A) (B) (C)		
/	3	(B)		
/	4	(B) (C)		
/	5	(B)		
/	1	(A) (B) (C)		
/	2	(A) (B) (C)		
/	3	(B)		
/	4	(B) (C)		
/	5	(B)		
/	1	(A) (B) (C)		

Objectives box:
- Pupils will add images into their presentations (S)
- Pupils will know what images are right in certain situations (K)
- Pupils will understand why an image has been put in and the advantage of having an image in a presentation (C)
- Pupils will copy and paste appropriate images from the internet into their presentations. (S)
- Pupils will work co-operatively in groups (A)

Evaluation:

Success measure – how do you know?
- Final Presentation

Final Presentation
Group Work

Group Work.

Final Presentations

Pupils exceeding objectives
- O.B .D.O

M.H. S.H

C.H

Class Management

Allocated groups before arrival.
Controlled transition

Actions

Made excellent contributions to discussion.
Praise.

Pupil Response

Pupils enjoyed group discussion activity.

Pupils not meeting objectives
- M.R.

Including images without purpose.

Own performance *in relation to previous targets*

Recording strategy proved to be a useful strategy to monitor contribution.

Actions
Speak to M.H about images next session.

Future targets *(Immediate/short/long term)*
Continue to develop questioning skills.

Notes:

Lesson: 3

Notes *including targeted questions*	Date: 12/3/03	Evaluation:
	Learning Outcomes *(SACK)/(a/w's)* Pupils will be able to:	Success measure - how do you know?
	To work productively when working individually (A) • Stay on task whilst working individually	Successful – observed the class, scanned the room and checked each pupil individually to see whether they were on task. If they didn't seem to be on task I went over to them to check.
	To design a leaflet on Page Plus 8 (S) Be able to design a tourist leaflet, including all the essential details of place, how to get there, weather conditions, attractions, where to stay.	All pupils, except Robyn, had started producing their leaflets on Page Plus 8 but didn't have enough time to finish them. Need to include time in next lesson.
Who are your audience? *Not sure she understand*	**To understand what makes a good leaflet (C)** Leaflet incorporates the following: • Suitable for intended audience • Clear layout - not too 'busy' • Good "flow" – the eye looks at each part in turn • Consistent use of colour • Careful use of white space • Good use of images	Most pupils can identify most of these points in question and answer sessions but are not applying them to their leaflets. Need to keep revisiting.
What makes a good leaflet? *Not sure she knows*	**To know the basics of Page Plus 8 (K)** • Be able to explain how to create a new publication • Be able to explain how to import images • Be able to explain how to import text • Be able to explain how to use the Word Art function in Page Plus 8	All selected pupils were able to explain how to use Page Plus 8 when asked.
	Attempt the extension task • Give pupil two paper designs of leaflets and ask them to write a short report on what they would change and why they would change it.	No-one started this task.
Missed elements out. *What do you need to include in your leaflet?* *What needs to be in the Analysis section of the reports?*	Pupils exceeding Outcomes • All pupils were working at different speeds and their work was of a different quality. • Pupils with high ability are Sue Wang and Nahida Sultana	Class Management • Arranged the room before the pupils arrived. • Settled the class before starting • Remind them to raise their hands when answering questions; • Asked name of pupils when answering questions or misbehaving. • Regularly scanned the room; • Circulated around the room; • Moved to pupils who didn't seem to be on task and checked their work. • Targeted pupils who were chatting, with questions.
Missed items out *What do you need to include in the leaflet?*	Actions • None needed. The quality of their work was higher however, the speed at which the task was completed was the same as the lower ability pupils.	Pupil Response • Pupils settled down fairly quickly when they arrived in the room. • Most pupils raised their hands to answer questions. • When approached, pupils chatting became quiet and got back on with the task. • Pupils soon realised that they could be asked a question and I found during the Q & A sessions most, if not all, pupils were listening.
	Pupils not meeting Outcomes • Gigi - does not speak good English – meeting outcomes but need to keep checking she is on task and understands what needs to be done.	Own performance *in relation to previous targets* More aware of pupils with their hands up and let them know that I have seen them. Scan the room more frequently.
What needs to be included in the Design section of the report?	Actions •	Future targets *(immediate/short/long term)* Classroom management issues: To be more aware of pupils with special needs. Keep checking on Gigi – English is not very good - make sure she is on task. Make sure choose different pupils to answer questions.

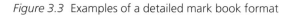

V2.1 © 2002 Liverpool JMU from an idea by Derek Kassem

Figure 3.3 Examples of a detailed mark book format

Where schools do not have discrete ICT in every year at KS3, or where they commence the teaching of KS4 courses early, additional strategies may be needed to ensure that the portfolio covers the breadth of evidence needed for deciding what level pupils have attained at KS3. In order to assist those teachers without immediate support in developing their levelling skills, the National Curriculum in Action website (see Websites at the end of this chapter) provides a variety of examples of levelled work.

From 2006, pupils have undertaken an online test to determine their level at KS3 (see Chapter 2). Although the test permits some adaptation the initial level entry point still needs to be determined by the teacher from class-based evidence.

Opportunities to assess and level should be taken at appropriate intervals throughout the whole 11–14 teaching period. Many successful schools operate a policy of mini-moderations (see later in this chapter) at the end of each unit of learning and teaching. It is also good practice to compare pupils' work with exemplar material, drawn from a number of sources, including examination bodies, and past work. It is a good idea to attend assessment training events and to take part in appropriate regional moderation events.

Activity 3.6 Judging the exemplar material

Your school should have a copy of the exemplar material. Try judging its level without reference to the supplied grades, and then compare your efforts with the grades provided for standardisation.

Do not be surprised that the results of the mini-moderations generate unexpected outcomes. It is often the case that pupils operate at higher levels in some areas of work than in others. When deciding an overall level you should use a 'best fit' model, but you must be able to justify your decision. You may report a pupil's attainment as being at a particular level but with elements of a higher level. This is particularly helpful for the pupil's next teacher as an aid in the planning process.

It is a useful exercise for pupils to participate in the levelling process to give them the level criteria (expressed in appropriate language) and ask them to try to identify where they might be on the scales.

Assessment should always be seen against the background of school, regional and national expectations and targets. Pupils should now arrive in secondary school with a wealth of data on their achievement to date. A number of analytical tools are routinely used by schools to predict the likely levels of pupils at 14 (and beyond). If used properly, these analytical tools can enhance the planning and execution of assessment.

It is particularly important that the levels being demonstrated by the learners are not limited by activity or opportunity. Although focusing on the National Curriculum for England, ideas to help you overcome this possible problem are provided by the DfES (2004a). Sometimes particular software packages do not help learners achieve high levels of decision-making, and the choice of resource may impact on achievement of higher grades.

For examination courses, the greater complexity of the assessment rules for the coursework mean it is even more important that this information is shared with the learners. If possible, a version close to that produced by the examination board should be in use at all times and modified to enable you to give feedback on how items can be improved before final submission. It may be useful for you to undertake some work as an assistant examiner during the early stages of your career in order to further gauge standards and how to advise your pupils so as to maximise their opportunities. It is also critical at this level to hold internal moderation sessions, using sample material when available or copies of work with a known grade from previous cohorts.

Activity 3.7 Assessment evidence for reports

A trainee teacher has been taking a class of 12 year olds for a whole term, and the class teacher has asked the trainee to produce some short reports for a parents' evening the following week (with only one more lesson before the event). If this were you, what assessment evidence would you be able to draw upon in order to write these reports?

_____

_____

_____

MODERATION

Moderation is the process during which groups of assessors agree common standards. Typically the body responsible for the external assessment will provide material that they have agreed a grade for. This will then be considered by the school assessing team, and their results compared with each other and with the assessment grades provided.

This process is an essential activity for teachers who are expected to grade pupil work as part of the assessment process. Often this activity will be supported by local authority (or similar) advisers to ensure that even small departments can be involved in this important form of professional development.

When schools use a variety of different teachers to deliver the subject in early secondary, it is also important that the ICT subject leader provides an opportunity for that delivery team to participate in internal moderation. This will ensure that the expectations on pupils are similar across the teaching team.

Activity 3.8 Participate in a moderation session

If it is possible, participate in a moderation session. Keep a note of how your standards compare with those of the rest of the team you work with.

ASSESSMENT FOR LEARNING

The Assessment for Learning (AfL) strategy developed in England by the Assessment Reform Group is one example of good practice in assessment.

We can define AfL as the process of gathering and interpreting appropriate evidence for use by pupils and their teachers to decide where the pupils have reached in their learning. You can determine from this what they need to attain and how best to reach their target.

- It is a core element of teaching and learning and is not an option that can be bolted on to an existing lesson structure.
- Learning goals should be shared with, and understood by, the pupils.
- It involves pupils in peer- and self-assessment.
- It provides 'next-steps' feedback whereby the pupil is praised for their achievement, shown their misconceptions and guided to improve their work.

Is there evidence that improving 'Assessment for Learning' raises standards? Is it actually practical to use AfL in the classroom? A variety of different research initiatives (the most famous being Black and Wiliam, 1998) have shown that effective formative assessment can indeed improve pupil performance at GCSE by one to two grades, and can raise pupils' predicted grades from the average level into the top 35% of achievement (in a criteria-based assessment model). This has been achieved in a wide range of schools.

Learning objectives must state clearly what the teacher intends the pupils to *learn*. They include references to knowledge, understanding, and skills developed in the lesson, and should link explicitly with learning outcomes and oral and written feedback.

There are simple acronyms to identify learning objectives and task outcomes. One example is: 'We Are Learning To' (lesson objectives) and 'What I'm Looking For' (task outcomes). These are often written as WALT and WILF.

> Assessment for learning depends crucially on teachers and pupils actually using the information gained to benefit future learning.
>
> (DfES, 2003)

Much current literature describes AfL; in particular, the resources for the ICT strand of the Secondary National Strategy in England include a substantial collection of materials. These are included in the *Whole School Development in Assessment for Learning* Pack (DfES, 2004b) which has subject-specific guidance included in the resources. In particular, Appendix 1.1 provides a succinct coverage of the research findings in the area.

Activity 3.9 Enhancing future performance

Choose an objective and the associated task outcomes from a lesson you recently taught. Translate these into language appropriate for pupils. Now write down, using similar language, four descriptors for the possible levels of outcome, structured to clearly indicate how the pupil might reach the next level above.

_____

_____

_____

_____

Key to AFL are the ideas that:

- Learners clearly understand what they are expected to do and learn.
- Feedback on learner performance is given promptly, and in a form that enables the learner to enhance future performance.
- Feedback is given in a positive manner, so that pupil self-esteem is supported.
- Assessment outlines are clearly understandable by the learner, so that they may attempt to self-assess when they have reached that level of maturity.
- Pupils are encouraged to take responsibility for their own learning process and begin to develop the skills for independent learning.

It is important to realise that AfL is central to, and concurrent with, a variety of different initiatives within a school. Figure 3.4 represents these linkages. It should be noted that linkages such as reporting and target-setting also have implications beyond the ICT department itself. AfL helps to gauge the ICT department's performance against school, local authority and national benchmarks. These benchmarks will include the national statistics

Figure 3.4 The inter-relationships within AfL

for each grade in external examinations at 14, 16 and 18, plus the equivalent statistics for the locality in which the school is situated. A department will be expected to be able to explain any discrepancy between their pupils' scores and these conflated statistics.

Feedback

Fundamental to the ideas of AfL is feedback. Part of the management issue with feedback is that, for it to be helpful, it needs to be comprehensive and positive. On many occasions you will find yourself repeating comments on many different pupil submissions. A well-thought-out proforma can aid the process by including comments that may be needed and which can be highlighted in some manner. This then leaves more time for adding the comments that may be unique to this learner.

It is always good practice for your feedback to indicate aspects of performance that have been done well, aspects of performance that fail to meet the requirements of the task, and the next steps to be undertaken. Feedback should always be positive and specific.

Activity 3.10 Writing useful feedback

Read this written feedback:

> 'This presentation is not what I was looking for. Try to improve it and then hand it in again.'

Is this appropriate and useful feedback? What would you write?

_____

_____

Oral feedback needs to be approached in a similar manner, providing positive encouragement where efforts are being successful in proceeding towards a good outcome, whilst providing suitable challenges to ensure that the learner operates at their best possible level. Where a pupil has not given a correct response, it is always useful to guide them towards a correct response rather than just being negative about what they said.

Activity 3.11 Revisiting your response

In Activity 3.2 you were asked to 'Consider a lesson that you have taught recently and try to identify the forms of assessment that you used in that lesson'. Revisit your response to that activity in the light of what you have now had a chance to think about.

SUMMARY

The importance of formative assessment in helping students to learn has been increasingly recognised over recent years. It is important to share the learning objectives with students and, when students are working on an activity, to focus their attention on the intended learning as well as the required product of the activity.

FURTHER READING

Black, P. and Wiliam, D. (1998) *Inside the Black Box*, London: Assessment Reform Group.

Black, P. and Harrison, C.(2001) 'Self- and peer-assesment and taking responsibility: the science student's role in formative assessment', *School Science Review* 83(302): 43–49, available at http://www.kcl.ac.uk/education/publications/SSR3.pdf, accessed Jan 2005.

DFES (2004) *Key Stage 3 National Strategy, Pedagogy and Practice Unit 12: Assessment for Learning*, London: DfES, available at http://www.standards.dfes.gov.uk/keystage3/respub/sec_pptl0, accessed June 2005.

Kennewell, S., Parkinson, J. and Tanner, H. (eds) (2003) *Learning to Teach ICT in the Secondary School*, London: RoutledgeFalmer: Chapter 7.

WEBSITES

Lewisham website:
http://www.lgfl.net/lgfl/leas/lewisham/communities/ICT/resources/Secondary/KS3/KS3.db_psc.

National Curriculum in Action website:
http://www.ncaction.org.uk/.

Chapter 4 The learning and teaching evaluation cycle

ANTHONY EDWARDS AND ANDREW CONNELL

INTRODUCTION

In this chapter we will look at the process of evaluation of teaching and learning: what evaluation is, why we evaluate, and how to evaluate lessons and longer-term plans. We will consider evaluation as part of a cyclical process involving planning, implementation and review at three levels.

By the end of this chapter you should be able to:

- use evaluation within the learning and teaching cycle to improve pupil learning and your teaching of ICT.

LESSON EVALUATION

What is a lesson evaluation?

A lesson evaluation is a critical reflection on the pupil experiences and the learning that took place during the lesson, together with an assessment of the impact of your teaching on that learning. It seeks to identify how you can develop your teaching in order to improve learning.

Note that pupils are central to this process. You need to analyse the quality of their work, behaviour, and responses. You also need to consider whether the objectives were met, and only then identify how your teaching contributed to their experience. An evaluation is *not* a narrative or diary account of what happened.

Why do we evaluate?

Lesson, medium-term and long-term plans all need to be evaluated. As a beginning teacher you may only be involved in evaluating lessons and medium-term plans.

- The reason you evaluate is to learn from your experiences in the classroom and become a better teacher.
- There is always something to learn from each of your lessons:

  - If you are to improve and progress, you need to analyse what went well to understand why, otherwise it is a chance performance and you may not be able to replicate it.
  - You need to analyse what went wrong, so that you can avoid the mistake in the future. Note that as a learner yourself, you have the right to make mistakes, but you may lose the right if you do nothing to avoid errors in the future.

- You will learn to use evaluations to set clear targets for the future, i.e. evaluations inform planning.
- Sometimes your evaluation of a lesson will raise questions and not provide the answers. It is still worth doing.

Evaluations are necessary for you to achieve improvement and progression. They are a useful tool to inform discussions with mentors and colleagues. As you progress in your career they will also help you with appraisal.

Figure 4.1 shows a good model of how evaluations can help to develop your competence in the classroom. Remember the acronym RIDE (Recollect, Identify, Develop and Explore). You can enter this sequence at any of the key points, but for ease of understanding we have numbered them. For more information on typical learning cycles for adults, see Kolb (1984).

How to evaluate lessons

The techniques outlined in this section focus on lesson evaluation. However, many of these concepts can also be applied to evaluation of medium-term and long-term plans. When evaluating, you should refer to the 'good practice' highlighted in Chapter 1.

A good evaluation should:

- describe, question and analyse the tasks which have gone well, as well as those that have not gone well;
- recognise your own learning;
- look forward and set yourself targets;
- consider what has happened and why it has happened;
- justify any judgements you make;

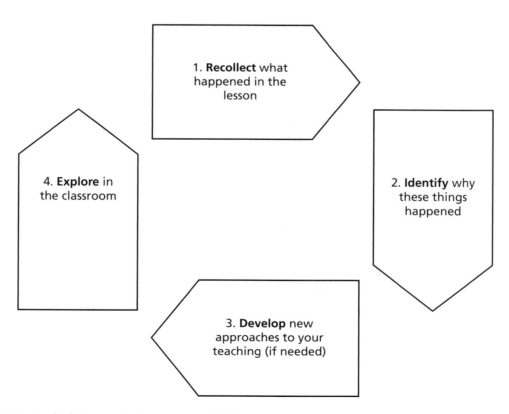

Figure 4.1 The lesson evaluation sequence (RIDE)

- provide evidence of careful thought, considering alternative explanations for an issue rather than jumping quickly to one explanation only;
- provide evidence on the quality of your teaching;
- recognise all factors that affect learning.

When to evaluate

Spend some time reflecting on a lesson as soon after the end of the lesson as possible. Try to do at least a rough evaluation for all morning lessons by the end of lunch, and for afternoon lessons before you leave school. If you leave it too long you forget the fine detail and how it felt, and the evaluation will be of less value. If you need to, you can go back to the day's rough notes later on that day.

Activity 4.1 A trainee's lesson evaluation

1 Read the following lesson evaluation undertaken by a trainee in the early stages of training. The context is a lesson on using a drawing package to create a Christmas card, with a mixed ability class who are in the second year of their secondary schooling.

The lesson was good. I enjoyed teaching how to manipulate text so that it could be distorted in shape, size and colour. I learnt how to do this properly when I did some work for a friend producing cards for her wedding-cake-making business. Most of the girls produced something, but they were hopeless at saving their work. Some of it was lost when we had a system failure towards the end of the lesson. I panicked at this point. I did not know what else I could do with them, without working computers. I asked Mr X, who was next door, if he had any fill-in activities. He was not very helpful even though I know he has some great ideas. When the system was restored, not all the work could be printed because I ran out of paper. I did not get on with child Y as usual. All he did was to shout out the wrong answer to the questions I asked. He was amongst a group of boys who were intent on disrupting the lesson, particularly when I was speaking to the whole class. They just did not want to work. I did well despite all the problems.

2 Make notes on the strengths and weaknesses of this evaluation.

_____

_____

_____

_____

What to think about when evaluating a lesson

Teaching has a direct impact on learning, but it will not be the only element you need to consider when evaluating. It is vital to start with what pupils have learned. You must ask yourself, did the pupils meet the learning objectives and how do you know this? The temptation, when evaluating, is to focus on your own performance as a teacher, but it should be a more complex process. You will need to take a number of other elements into consideration. The relationship between the elements is illustrated in Figure 4.2.

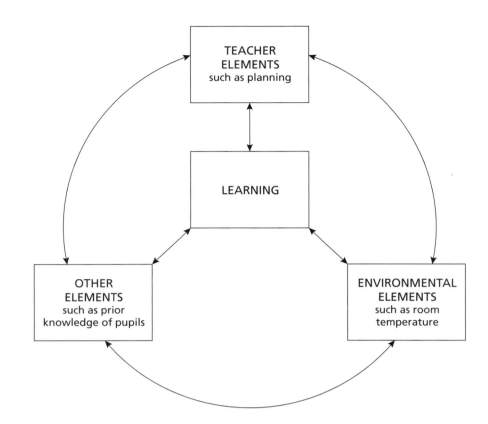

Figure 4.2 Factors affecting learning

You will note that all the elements are interlinked and may have a bearing on each other.

Activity 4.2 Factors affecting learning

Using the three elements from Figure 4.2 (Teacher, Environment and Other) as separate headings, make a list of factors that have affected learning for some of the teaching you have undertaken or observed.

Teacher   Environment   Other
_____   _____   _____
_____   _____   _____
_____   _____   _____
_____   _____   _____
_____   _____   _____
_____   _____   _____

Some possible answers are provided at the end of this chapter.

Here are some questions to consider when evaluating:

*   **What were you pleased about?** Think about your feelings.
*   **Were the planned learning objectives achieved?** How do you know? If not, why not? (See Chapter 1.)
*   **What was the feedback from other adults in the lesson?** It may be formal, e.g. a

written observation of the lesson, or more often, informal. Both are important. You need to reflect on what is said, but be aware of people's expertise in lesson evaluation. There may be significant differences in what they think and what you think. This is not necessarily a problem as long as you can consider the question 'why are there differences?' It is very important to have a dialogue with some people, particularly your subject mentor.

- **What does the planned assessment that took place during the lesson tell you about learning?** Did the pupils make progress? How much? How do you know? If not, why not? (See Chapter 3.)
- **What does the informal assessment that took place during the lesson tell you about the learning?** Did the pupils make progress? How much? How do you know? If not, why not?
- **What was the feedback (formal and informal) from pupils?** What can you learn from the way pupils responded or behaved or from their body language? Did misbehaviour occur because of what you did? Did they enjoy the lesson? If so, why? If not, why not? Of course, not all aspects of their work need to be enjoyable, so consider whether they enjoyed parts of the lesson, and why.
- **How effective was your organisation?** Did you get to the classroom on time? Did you have resources such as handouts ready? Did you distribute them effectively? Did you check that the computers worked?
- **Were there any external factors that influenced the quality of your lesson?** Was behaviour affected by events before the lesson? Was the lesson interrupted?
- **Were there any environmental factors that influenced the quality of the lesson?** Was the temperature in the room too high or too low? Was the noise outside the room distracting? (See Chapter 2.)
- **How effective were the differentiation strategies you used?** (See Capel *et al.* (2005), Unit 4.1.) Did you meet the needs of every pupil? How do you know?
- **Was your questioning effective?** Did you plan your questions? Did you mix open and closed questions? Did you target some pupils? How did pupils respond to questioning? Were they all involved? (See Capel *et al.* (2005), Unit 2.1; Kennewell *et al.* (2003), Chapters 5 and 6.)
- **How good were your communication skills?** Did you use appropriate vocabulary, give clear instructions and demonstrations, choose examples well? Did you use the technology effectively, e.g. interactive whiteboard?
- **Did you manage the class effectively?** (See Capel *et al.* (2005), Unit 3.3.) What interventions were used and how effective were they? Do you need to target particular pupils next lesson?
- **Was the lesson well-paced?** (See Capel *et al.* (2005), Unit 2.1.) Did the pace vary? Were your planned timings realistic? Why? Or why not?
- **Were the pupils interested/motivated during the lesson?** For how much of the lesson were pupils on task? Was the amount of work produced appropriate? Were they only interested in parts of the lesson?
- **Were transitions managed effectively?** Did you signal these clearly? Did pupils move between computers and desks safely? Did they engage in new tasks quickly?
- **What evidence was there of pupil errors and misconceptions?** Did you pay good attention to these and try to remedy them? Do you need to address any errors next lesson?
- **Were there any surprises?** What were they, and can you anticipate them next time?
- **Was it necessary to change your plan during the lesson?** Why?
- **What notes or points for the next lesson do you need?** For example, who to target with questions, who missed the lesson, who owes homework?
- **What would you change if you had to do this lesson again?**
- **Did the lesson cover the teaching standards you targeted, or any other standards?** How do you know?

Activity 4.3 Your five key questions

It is unlikely you will have the time immediately after a lesson to reflect on and answer all the questions listed above. You will probably need to do rough summary notes and come back to them later. Produce a set of five key questions for the rough notes that will allow you to fully evaluate later.

_____

_____

_____

_____

_____

Activity 4.4 A more useful lesson evaluation?

After reading the section above, review the alternative evaluation below, written for the lesson described earlier in the chapter. Is this evaluation more useful?

On the whole I was disappointed with this lesson. I made a number of basic errors that spoilt what I considered to be a promising activity. However, I was pleased that I was clearly able to explain how to manipulate text. I used appropriate technical language, my instructions were clear and the technology (interactive whiteboard) worked.

Not all the pupils were able to use the desktop publishing package comfortably. I did not prepare enough support materials to cope with the wide range of abilities in the class. This meant that I had to spend a long time supporting a few, at the expense of the majority.

I was only able to base my assessment on the responses to my question-and-answer session because a system failure meant that I was unable to review each pupil's work at their computer. The questions I asked were not very varied. Most only required a one-word answer, although it was clear that a small group of pupils understood the techniques I had previously explained to them. I could not offer any more detailed analysis than this because lack of paper for the printer and unsaved work limited what I could assess.

The boys seemed to be less engaged in the theme. They liked working on the computers (the speed with which they moved once I told them to log on was amazing) but spent no time thinking about design issues. I think that both the structure of the lesson and the nature of the activities were inappropriate for their needs.

The lesson stalled when the system failed for about fifteen minutes. I did not know what to do and tried to consult Mr X who was next door for help. He unfortunately had his own issues to deal with (difficult class and no computers) and could not help. Leaving the classroom only made the situation worse and I had to struggle to regain control. When the system was restored there was too little time left to do anything meaningful.

I was surprised by a number of things – the system failure, the lack of a routine for saving work and the fact that there was little paper for the printer. I could not anticipate the first but should have been more alert to the other two.

Activity 4.4 *continued*

> *I will do the following:*
>
> 1) *Differentiate more accurately – in terms of broadening the theme to provide scope for different approaches and interests, and creating additional support material for different ability levels.*
> 2) *Prepare an additional activity to cover potential equipment failure.*
> 3) *Target initial assessment on the small group of boys who did not participate fully in this lesson so that I can determine what they do know accurately and quickly.*

EVALUATION TEMPLATES

In the early stages of your career you may find it helpful to use a template such as the one in Table 4.1.

Table 4.1 Lesson evaluation template

LESSON EVALUATION
CLASS_____ DATE_____
What progress did all/most/some pupils make in learning? Consider each learning objective (LO):
LO1
LO2
LO3
What do you need to revisit, consolidate, revise, move on to with this class in the next lesson?
What were you *pleased* about after the lesson?
Specific class-management issues/organisatonal issues that need to be addressed:

A good lesson evaluation template should:

- be easy to use;
- be understandable to you;
- be understandable by others;
- have a suitable layout; for instance, avoiding boxes of fixed size since some questions need more detailed answers than others (so an electronic table will be ideal).

Activity 4.5 Produce your own template

Review the template in Table 4.1 and produce your own template that you can use to evaluate lessons.

Evaluating for the more experienced trainee teacher

As you gain more experience, you may be able to move away from the structured evaluation formats used by a beginning teacher. Whatever format you choose to use, it should cover the following four points:

1 What were the positive aspects of the lesson, and how do you know this?
2 Were the lesson objectives met, and how do you know?
3 Were there any development issues arising from the lesson, and how do you know?
4 What have I learnt about the theme? (See below.)

USING A THEME

The final part of the evaluation, mentioned above, will be a reflection on one particular aspect of the lesson that would be useful. This may be a theme agreed with a mentor or appraiser, or may arise from issues raised in a previous evaluation, or it may be something that would be additionally helpful for your development.

The theme may be different for each class, or may be the same for several classes. Examples might be:

- Look for more subtle issues, such as differences between individual pupils' learning.
- Concentrate on one part of a lesson or an issue, such as transition points from whole class to individual work.
- Identify an ongoing issue with a class, such as repeated misbehaviour, and use this as a focus for a sequence of evaluations.
- Compare the same issue in different classes, for instance exploring why a technique works better with one group of pupils than with another.

Other themes could be about:

- use of more open questions;
- targeting questions to challenge the able;
- use of praise;
- strategies for supporting a particular pupil;
- use of starters or plenaries;
- differentiation;
- assessment;
- oral feedback;
- tracking coursework during lessons;
- use of your voice and body language.

It may also be useful, if you have parallel classes, e.g. two classes doing the same unit, to make the focus a comparison of the two lessons and produce one overall evaluation for both lessons.

Activity 4.6   Using a theme

Look at your own evaluations, identify a theme and build it into future evaluations.

EVALUATING MEDIUM-TERM AND LONG-TERM PLANS

Evaluating an unfamiliar scheme of work

Before using a scheme of work for a topic, you should consider the following questions:

- Is it clearly linked to the statutory requirements for ICT?
- Does it provide help to plan differentiated lessons?
- Has it got clear learning objectives?
- Does it clearly link suggested activities and outcomes to learning objectives?
- Does it suggest how learning objectives may be assessed?
- Does it include opportunities to support cross-curricular themes?
- Does it have realistic suggested times for each 'unit'?
- Does it promote good teaching practice?
- Will it motivate the pupils?
- Is it flexible?
- Does it identify resources?
- Are the resources appropriate?

- Is the sequence sensible?
- Does it have a good balance between knowledge, skills and understanding?
- Does it prepare pupils for the 'real world'?
- Does it use a range of ICT tools? Are they sufficiently up-to-date?
- Does it promote independent learning?
- Does it take into account pupils' experiences?
- Does it promote group work?
- Does it encourage a creative approach?

If you have concerns about any particular aspects, it is advisable to discuss them with your mentor or head of department. They should be able to clarify the ideas in the scheme of work, or suggest alternatives for your particular class.

Evaluating your own scheme of work

When you have the opportunity to develop a scheme of work for yourself, a cyclical evaluation process is appropriate (see Figure 4.3).

Remember the acronym LIME (Look, Identify, Modify and Explore).

1   If you are to improve your plan to promote better learning and progress, you need to analyse what went well and understand why.
2   You need to analyse what was unsuccessful so that you can avoid the same mistakes in the future; for instance, if the scheme timings were unrealistic then they need to be adjusted.

Some of the techniques used to evaluate a lesson can be applied to evaluating a scheme of work. However, there are a number of differences in the process because of:

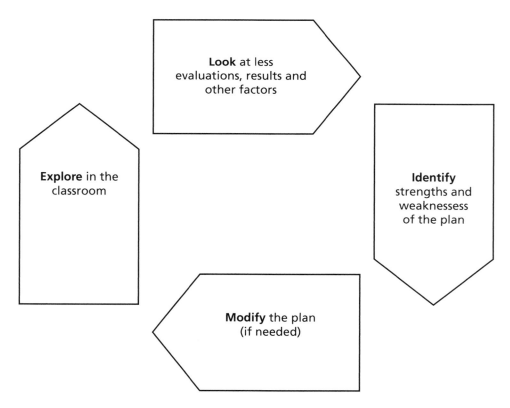

Figure 4.3 The medium-term and long-term plan evaluation sequence (LIME)

- The scale of the undertaking: there is a much bigger evidence base.
- The frequency with which it done: perhaps twice a year.
- The nature of the evidence used to evaluate. This may include:

  - Lesson evaluations from every lesson associated with the scheme
  - Results and assessment (internal and external) of the pupils
  - The match between resources and the delivery of the scheme
  - Department review meetings
  - Pupil feedback
  - Other sources.

By analysing the evidence identified above in conjunction with the questions listed at the start of this section, you can evaluate your plan effectively.

Activity 4.7   Evaluating one of your plans

Having read this section, evaluate one of your medium-term plans.

_____

_____

_____

_____

THE LEARNING AND TEACHING CYCLE

The learning and teaching cycle is the link between lesson planning and medium-term and long-term planning. You need to determine how effective this link is. For you, this task is difficult because each phase operates in a different time frame and, with the advent of schemes of work developed by a range of agencies (government and exam boards) there is less opportunity to do medium-term and long-term planning. Nevertheless, it is still important to evaluate how well integrated they are. Figure 4.4 clearly identifies how the phases are related and indicates that you cannot evaluate in isolation.

Activity 4.2

Some possible answers to Activity 4.2 Factors affecting learning

Teacher	Environment	Other
Planning	_Temperature_	_Pupil behaviour_
Teaching style	_Noise levels_	_Activities prior to lesson_
Pace	_Lighting_	_Time of the day_
Subject knowledge	_Room layout_	_Proximity of lesson to holiday_

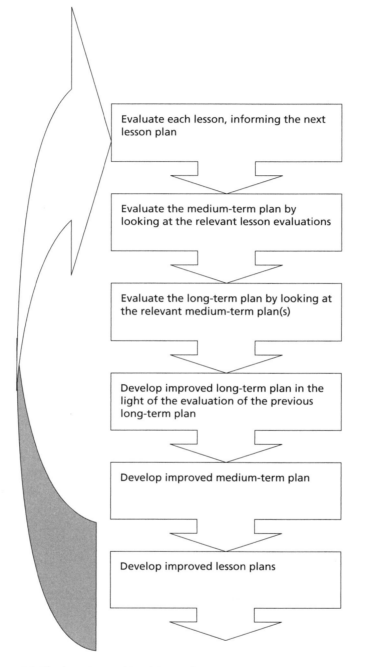

Figure 4.4 The learning and teaching cycle

SUMMARY

The importance of systematic evaluation of your teaching was highlighted at the end of Chapter 1, and we have now considered strategies for carrying this out at different levels. During your initial experiences of teaching, you will focus on your own performance, but this should shift towards a focus on the pupils' learning. In parallel with this, your analysis should develop from consideration of individual lessons to evaluation of student progress over longer timescales and the evidence that you need to be confident about your effectiveness in ensuring this progress.

FURTHER READING

Capel, S., Leask, M. and Turner, T. (2002) *Learning to Teach in the Secondary School*, London: RoutledgeFalmer, Unit 5.4, Improving your teaching.

Florian, L. and Hegarty, J. (eds) (2004) *ICT and Special Educational Needs*, Buckingham: Open University Press.

Forsyth, I. and Jolliffe, A. (1999) *Evaluating a Course: Practical Strategies for Teachers, Lecturers and Trainers*, London: Kogan Page.

Kennewell, S. (2004) *Meeting the Standards in using ICT for Secondary Teaching*, London: RoutledgeFalmer (particularly p. 113).

Kyriacou, C. (2001) *Essential Teaching Skills*, Cheltenham: Nelson Thornes, Chapter 8, Reflection and evaluation.

Kolb, D. A. (1984) *Experiential Learning: Experience as the Source of Learning and Development*, New Jersey: Prentice-Hall.

Stephens, P. and Crawley, T. (2002) *Becoming an Effective Teacher*, Cheltenham: Nelson Thornes.

WEBSITES

Subject leader checklist for evaluation of departmental teaching:
http://www.bcs.org/NR/rdonlyres/53E21D11-5300-413E-917C-3F363A79E006/0/subjectchecklist.pdf.

Example of an evaluation proforma:
http://www.teachernet.gov.uk/growingschools/downloads/Rabbits%20Lesson%20Plan.DOC.

Success criteria:
http://www.teachernet.gov.uk/supplyteachers/detail.cfm?&vid=4&cid=16&sid=99&ssid=4020607&opt=sectionfocus.

Part 2   Themes in ICT teaching

This section provides a variety of ideas for enhancing your teaching of ICT, and presents the ICT curriculum thematically as an alternative to the structure of the National Curriculum in England and the examination board syllabuses. It covers the same scope and depth of ICT knowledge, skills and understanding, but incorporates some of the current thinking about curriculum themes, including thinking skills and personalised learning, which will influence future schemes of work in schools.

Chapter 5 develops the theme of creativity, a theme much neglected in England since the advent of the National Curriculum. It examines the role of ICT capability as a foundation for the inventiveness and imagination that characterise creativity, considers how ICT affects the concept of creativity itself, and provides ideas concerning how creativity can be implemented within the ICT curriculum.

Chapter 6 examines the theme of prediction, which is new and relatively under-developed as a strand running through the curriculum. One reason for this is the difficulty presented by traditional media such as books and pens in carrying out activities where pupils look for patterns in data, make meaning of their findings, put forward conjectures, test them out and evaluate the results. The provisional nature of ICT outputs ensures that it is now possible to devise a fresh set of curriculum activities that can support the learning of new ideas, as well as learning old things in new ways.

In Chapter 7, one of the original strands of ICT capability, communicating information, is brought up to date. This does not mean that the activities suggested are all new; some of them were developed in the 1980s, but limited and unreliable ICT resources restricted their adoption by teachers. The time is now right for more use of ICT to support drafting and editing processes, decision-making activities and collaborative working in the classroom.

Chapter 8 is linked to all the others, but has an independent theme of exploration. In exploratory work, the feedback feature of ICT is exploited in order to provide activities which are structured for learning purposes yet allow pupils to take risks and 'play' within a safe environment which they enjoy navigating. Exploring and taking measured risks seems to be important for learning – indeed, for success in life – and the chapter shows how ICT can help shift the balance of control of learning towards the pupil.

Chapter 5 Creativity

CATHY WICKENS

INTRODUCTION

In this chapter we will look at:

- Why ICT capability is needed to be creative.
- What technology can bring to the concept of creativity.
- How creativity can be fostered in the classroom.
- How creativity can be developed through targeted activities in school.

By the end of this chapter you should be able to:

- understand the concept of creativity and its key position in the ICT curriculum;
- use your imagination to produce innovative, exciting ideas for teaching and learning.

CREATIVITY AND ICT

Creativity is not usually associated with ICT; it is more likely to be linked with Art, Drama or Music. The perception of the nature of ICT as being a technology that has the right answers, however, leads pupils to make assumptions that there is only one possible outcome to an ICT task. This chapter explores the concept of creativity in ICT, arguing that it probably encompasses many or all of the other features of ICT and pushes the boundaries of what is possible with the use of technology. The roles of audience and author become blurred. Examples can be found particularly in multimedia work and web authoring. The integration of text, graphics, sound, video and hyperlinks allows the reader to take 'excursions' into the narrative, exploring, researching, exchanging information and learning as they do so. This could also apply to developing computer-based solutions to problems, such as work with databases where pupils are given the freedom to pursue possibilities and are encouraged to 'think outside the box'.

Creativity is characterised by inventiveness and the use of imagination. Craft (2001) differentiates between those with 'big C creativity' such as Einstein, Bach and Picasso, and the potential in all of us for developing 'little c creativity', or 'possibility thinking', as an essential life skill. A report entitled 'All Our Futures: Creativity, Culture and Education' argues that a national strategy for creative and cultural education is essential

> . . . to unlock the potential of every young person in order for them to have the oppor-
> tunity to contribute to the country's economic prosperity and social cohesion . . . there
> is an important relationship between creative and cultural education, which in turn has

significant implications for methods of teaching and assessment, the balance of the school curriculum and for partnerships between schools and the wider world.

(NACCCE, 1999: 6)

The UK government has responded to this need by funding a number of projects over the past few years.

Whilst the importance of creativity has already been recognised by researchers for some years, the National Curriculum in Action website (see Websites at the end of this chapter) is a useful place for you to begin background reading. But for a more detailed understanding, you should look at *Literature Review in Creativity, New Technologies and Learning* (Loveless, 2002). Reading this material suggests that the more we understand about intellectual ability and the way we learn, the more we realise that creativity is not the privilege of the few but can be experienced by all.

WHY CAPABILITY IS NEEDED TO BE CREATIVE

ICT capability concerns transferable learning rather than focusing on basic skills or techniques, and Kennewell *et al.* (2003: 7) suggest that it needs five key components: routines, techniques, key concepts, processes, and higher order skills and knowledge. Loveless and Wegerif (2004) look at the relationship between capability, the five strands of the ICT National Curriculum and the characteristics of creativity to conclude that,

it is not access to ICT that 'delivers' creativity but the opportunities such access can afford.

Loveless and Wegerif (2004: 96)

Therefore to allow for creativity to blossom, and for pupils to use their developing ICT capability, the planning should be in educational settings which involve:

- thinking and behaving imaginatively
- purposeful activity
- generating something original to the individual
- outcomes which are of value in relation to the objective.

(QCA, 2005)

CASE STUDY: KNOCK-KNOCK JOKES

A Year 7 project challenged pupils to create a presentation based on knock-knock jokes (for stimulus material, see Further reading at the end of this chapter). They searched the internet for suitable jokes which they then copied on to a series of slides. This was followed by a discussion on the concept of audience (their peers) and how they could develop humour in the presentation, using, for example, animation and sound. Pupils were encouraged to work autonomously, using capability developed in previous units, planning first on paper and using peer-assessment as they refined their presentations. Towards the end of the project they were asked to evaluate their work, starting with group and then peer evaluation as a stimulus.

COMMENTARY ON CASE STUDY

There are several potential barriers to learning when Key Stage 3 pupils work on this type of activity. Skimming and scanning of websites and the selection of appropriate text is difficult for those with low literacy levels. In addition, the concept of audience can be challenging for pupils of this age, and the highest-order thinking skill, evaluation, can be difficult for most pupils to do well. In this project, pupils use websites intended for their age range and an audience of their peers, with a focus of humour, which makes it a highly accessible context. Class teacher Lee O'Neill commented that 'throughout the unit all of the lessons seemed to include a lot of laughter and really focused learning, but the sessions using peer-assessment and formative feedback and the final evaluation were the highlights. The context seemed to allow pupils the freedom to evaluate in far more detail than usual – not only what they had done, but also why and how. All pupils succeeded with a credible outcome but many achieved considerably beyond their target level of attainment.'

Csikszentmihalyi (1996) uses the term 'flow' to describe situations where people are so focused that they move effortlessly from one element to another. He classifies nine elements which this type of activity provides:

- clear goals;
- immediate feedback;
- balance between challenges and skills;
- merging of action and awareness;
- elimination of distractions;
- lack of fear of failure;
- lack of self-consciousness;
- distortion of sense of time;
- enjoyment for its own sake.

It could be argued that there is a tension between allowing the pupils to stay with the 'flow', or breaking it with what the teacher perceives as useful intervention. For example, there may be a tension between the need to maintain the timing of the lesson and the need to discuss errors and misconceptions. Csikszentmihalyi describes the teachers or 'knowledgeable others' who control the situation as 'gatekeepers' who nurture the creative development of individuals. Therefore the challenge at the planning stage is to recognise the needs of individuals, anticipate intervention and plan carefully so that targeted but flexible support is offered.

This project used presentation software but the principles could equally apply to multimedia authoring, using, for example, Mediator (www.matchware.net) or Opus Presenter (www.digitalworkshop.com).

Activity 5.1 Creative use of ICT

1 Explore the potential of usual classroom software by experimenting with tools and techniques in a different way, thus challenging your own creativity. For example, using the symmetry work by Escher as a stimulus (http://www.mcescher.com/), create your own drawing using Microsoft Publisher. Switch off the grid so that you can produce a sophisticated result, use grouping, re-sizing, flipping, etc.

2 Think about the links with numeracy and tesselation, and evaluate the possible outcome against the QCA (2005) guidelines listed previously.

3 When evaluating a teaching episode see if you observe any of the nine characteristics of 'flow' listed above, and think about why this happened.

4 Reflect on any creative use of ICT you observed on your primary school placement, or read Wheeler (2005). What issues are there for transition from one key stage to another that the Knock-Knock jokes case study overcame?

WHAT TECHNOLOGY CAN BRING TO THE CONCEPT OF CREATIVITY

The next scenario makes connections between school, home, communities of learning and the potential that technology can offer. First, consider the features of the actual software and hardware available:

- Provisionality – which allows the user to model, make changes;
- Interactivity – immediate and dynamic feedback;
- Capacity and range – for example vast amounts of global information;
- Speed and automatic functions – allowing for higher-order thinking of synthesis and analysis.

(Based on TTA, 1998)

Consider what other affordances may be provided as developments in technology mean that interactive whiteboards are becoming commonplace, and technologies such as scanners, digital cameras (still and video), webcams, and data logging equipment are also readily available.

The Impact2 report (Becta, 2002) suggests that pupils are already engaging at a high level of creativity within their own world of mobile phones, MP3 players and playstations. However the report goes on to say that pupils associate 'learning' with school-related use, and they typically describe all ICT use at home as 'games'. But, when questioned further it appears that they are still learning in their leisure pursuits, including factual knowledge and conceptual understanding.

CASE STUDY: SCIENCE WEEK

Swavesey Village College, a science specialist comprehensive school in Cambridgeshire, wanted to have a whole-school activity for 'science week' which would raise the profile of science and stimulate the pupils' interest beyond the curriculum. Incubated chicken eggs were timed to hatch at the start of the week, and the chicks then became the focus for the remainder of the week. The science club used desktop publishing to promote the event, and daily updates and bulletins during the week were published on the school website. A webcam was placed above the incubator, and images were beamed on to an interactive whiteboard in the science lab. A large monitor in the school reception also displayed the events. Once the eggs had all hatched, the webcam was moved to the brooder.

Figure 5.1 Chickens at Swavesey Village College, Cambridgeshire

---

COMMENTARY ON CASE STUDY

What was physically a very small project became accessible to the whole school with the use of very simple technology, and was transformed into an engaging interactive experience. Deputy Head of Science, Rebecca Gooding, was overwhelmed with the response from both pupils and colleagues who chose a range of ways to interact with the activites. Some emailed questions and comments, others chose to come and look directly, whilst all observed the beamed images during the course of the week. 'The pupils were so creative – whilst I set up the incubating eggs and the webcam the rest of the ideas such as posters and the website all came from the children.' The ease with which the pupils used the technology demonstrates that they must have had the necessary capability, but also that it was highly accessible.

It could be argued that the pupils did not have the 'flow' described previously, but perhaps the phenomenon was a little less obvious in that the pupils were doing this on their own or in small groups. This social practice where creativity is fostered through interaction and communication within their community is explored by Bruner (1996) who recognised that collaboration with an 'expert' offers children the opportunities to work with others and generate ideas. In this case the stimulus was offered by the teacher and the chicks, but increasingly schools are using, for example, artists, poets, or actors in residence, or even virtual communities, where pupils maybe work with peers from other schools or ask questions from online experts. Visit the Interactive Education Project (see Websites at the end of this chapter) to see a range of projects.

Activity 5.2   ICT across the curriculum

Teachers of ICT are frequently asked to work outside their subject specialism, such as organising INSET on new software or advising on curriculum development.

1   If they are available to you, look at the 'ICT across the Curriculum' materials from the National Strategy (DfES, 2004e). Do you consider that the ideas and guidance are likely to promote creativity or can you think of ways that you would adapt them? Discuss and share your ideas with colleagues from other subject areas.
2   Look at your own teaching space. What can you do to promote creativity? Walk round the school to get inspiration for good practice in display work.

HOW CREATIVITY CAN BE FOSTERED IN THE CLASSROOM

The typical ICT classroom with rows of anonymous computers does not seem conducive to creative experiences but, short of spending vast amounts of money, you will have to be resourceful and imaginative within your traditional setting. Therefore the physical learning environment needs to be redesigned to support creativity by providing accessible resources and stimulating displays (see Chapter 2). As an example, visit Highwire, a City Learning Centre which was designed as a creative space (see Websites at the end of this chapter).

In the first two case studies we can see examples of 'little c creativity' taking place, but the secondary school timetable is not conducive to creativity (Pollard, 2005). 'On Monday period 3 and then for the next five lessons you will all be creative' exclaims the teacher: premeditated creativity is not inspiring! That does not imply that planning for creativity cannot happen, but the reflective practitioner needs to be aware of opportunities that could arise and react to them. Furthermore, Lucas (2001) asserts that teachers' respect for individual learners is crucial for underpinning creativity (see the Campaign for Learning in Websites at the end of this chapter).

CASE STUDY: INCREASING PARTICIPATION

A teacher of GCSE ICT used discussion to develop understanding of the effects of ICT on society, but she was aware that she had some members of the class who were reluctant to join in. She already used a virtual learning environment (VLE – see Websites at the end of this chapter) where she posted resources for pupils to access, which she decided to extend by opening the discussion board. She invited the pupils to discuss the issues online, first in the classroom and then as a homework activity.

COMMENTARY ON CASE STUDY

The teacher was surprised that those who didn't participate in face-to-face discussion still didn't offer much when they were using the VLE in class. However once they were on their own with time to reflect, they offered creative and imaginative responses. 'Pupils tended to write more than usual, were often witty, used language appropriately and I was surprised at some of the timings of their postings, such as early Saturday evening. I felt that the pupils were learning from each other and would definitely use the forum again when teaching this topic or similar ones.'

We have already looked at the teaching space, but in addition we need to look beyond the physical to the virtual environment. Use of VLEs such as Moodle (a free open-source management system – see Websites at the end of this chapter), allows pupils to interact with resources, ask questions and gain feedback beyond the classroom. In this scenario the teacher reacted to the needs of the few, which in turn has supported the whole group. The use of asynchronous discussion in this case created a virtual community of learning. The 'flow' was not seen as the pupils worked in isolation, but there was a trail of ideas left for all in the group to learn from and for the teacher to mediate and give feedback.

Activity 5.3 VLEs and discussion groups

1   If you are not already using a VLE, then look at Moodle (for example) and trial it with one unit that you are teaching. Post resources and open the discussion board, if appropriate. If you are already using a VLE, discover what tools you are not already using and trial these with your pupils.
2   Look on the internet for one of the thousands of discussion groups that you can join. Reflect on the experience: did you react differently in a virtual space?

HOW CREATIVITY CAN BE DEVELOPED THROUGH TARGETED ACTIVITIES IN SCHOOL

There is a tension between introducing skills and creating imaginative authentic contexts for teaching when developing ICT capability. In this section we look at the use of targeted activities and modelling approaches to learning.

We touched on the notion of feedback to pupils in the last case study, but have yet to consider how assessment for learning (formative assessment) can support creativity. *All our Futures* (NACCCE,1999) and the work of Black and Wiliam (1998) suggest that formative feedback is particularly important in supporting creative teaching and learning and should conform to four principles:

- It must be built into the design of the teaching programme as an integral element rather than added on to it.
- Pupils should be actively involved in the processes of assessment and contribute to them.
- It must be focused on the development of each individual: i.e., it must be criterion referenced rather than norm referenced.
- The evidence it provides must be acted on if teaching is to be tuned to the range of pupils' individual developments.

NACCCE (1999: 131)

We can see that this was an integral part of the first case study and in this final one we will see that as a result of feedback the teacher alters his medium-term plan to produce a targeted activity.

CASE STUDY: PRODUCING THE IMAGINATIVE RESPONSE

A teacher of a GCE ICT group was frustrated by the lack of creativity from his pupils when engaging with their coursework (A2 Module 6: Use of information systems for problem solving). He felt that whilst they were competent at analysing the needs of their user groups they had little imagination practically. He decided that an understanding of Visual Basic for Applications (VBA) would allow them to create a bespoke soloution but he also felt that they needed some light relief from their projects. After a simple introduction, linking existing knowledge of macros to the potential of VBA, he set them the challenge of producing a simple game in either Access or Excel. The range of response varied from noughts and crosses to Blockbusters, but what is most important is that the pupils developed their ICT capability, and the resultant coursework demonstrated the flair and imaginative response that had previously been lacking.

COMMENTARY ON THE CASE STUDY

The constraints of the secondary and post-16 curriculum, with deadlines of coursework, examinations, a strict timetable and performance tables, inevitably deter teachers from moving away from what they feel has to be taught. Time is felt to be the main issue, but it may be that a targeted activity as described above can save time in the long run. It models the creative approach within a safe context. What the teacher realised is that:

> there can be a positive interaction between creativity, ICT capability and the features of digital technologies that offers learners and teachers opportunites to work in new and different ways.

Loveless and Wegerif (2004: 101)

Activity 5.4 Using new software

1   Whilst most of the pupils in the case study were competent at analysis, it is often useful to use concept maps and computer-based mapping tools such as Inspiration (see 'Software' at the end of this chapter) to represent the issues and ideas visually. Try doing this with one of your classes, either in small groups or as a class, using an interactive whiteboard.

Activity 5.4 *continued*

2 Using software such as Camtasia Studio or Screencorder you can record demonstrations of techniques and skills, including your own commentary; these can then be used for targeted activities, frequently needed by only a few pupils.

SUMMARY

The main theme that has run throughout this chapter focused on the role of the teacher and how, in order to foster creativity using ICT, they need to be discerning about how they:

- develop ICT capability;
- use the the physical or virtual learning environment;
- allow for playfulness, humour, failure, originality;
- plan, including assessment for learning;
- use authentic and purposeful contexts;
- realise the potential of the technology;
- realise the potential of individuals.

FURTHER READING

Boden, M. (2004) *The Creative Mind: Myths and Mechanisms*, London: Routledge.

Claxton, G. and Lucas, B. (2004) *Be Creative: Essential Steps to Revitalize Your Work and Life*, London: BBC.

Cowley, S. (2004) *Getting the Buggers to Think*, London: Continuum.

Craft, A., Jeffrey, B. and Leibling, M. (eds) (2001) *Creativity in Education*, London: Continuum.

Csikszentmihalyi, M. (1996) *Creativity: Flow and the Psychology of Discovery and Invention*, New York: HarperCollins.

Loveless, A. (2002) *Literature Review in Creativity, New Technologies and Learning*, Bristol: Futurelab. Available at <http://www.futurelab.org.uk/download/pdfs/research/lit_reviews/Creativity-Review.pdf> (accessed 9 November 2006).

Fisher, R., and Williams, M. (eds) (2004) *Unlocking Creativity: Teaching Across the Curriculum*, London: David Fulton.

NACCCE (1999) *All our Futures: Creativity, Culture and Education*, Sudbury: DfEE.

WEBSITES

National Curriculum in Action: *Creativity, find it, promote it*: www.ncaction.org.uk/creativity

Knock-Knock jokes: www.knock-knock-joke.com

Escher: www.mcescher.com

Interactive Education Project: www.interactiveeducation.ac.uk

Highwire CLC: www.highwire.org.uk

Virtual Learning Environments: ferl.becta.org.uk/display.cfm?page=248

Moodle: www.moodle.org

Campaign for Learning: www.compaign-for-learning.org.uk.

SOFTWARE

Mediator: www.matchware.net

Opus Presenter: www.digitalworkshop.com

Inspiration: www.inspiration.org
Camtasia Studio: www.camtasiastudio.com
Screencorder: www.matchware.net.

Chapter 6 Prediction

JOHN WOOLLARD

INTRODUCTION

In this chapter we will look at the ways in which you can use ICT in the classroom to support *hypotheses* and *predictions* and how modern technology is enabling: *pattern seeking, extrapolation* and *interpolation* to meet the challenges of the information explosion of the twenty-first century.

We will attempt to answer the following questions:

1 How can we use pattern and prediction activities in the classroom?
2 How can pupils make sense and draw information from a mass of data?
3 What capabilities do our pupils need, to analyse and predict effectively?
4 What facilities does technology bring to summarising and communicating the patterns found in data?
5 How can we develop our pupils' ability to predict through targeted activities based upon curriculum- and subject-specific models and simulations?

By the end of this chapter you should be able to:

- see the potential for using more activities requiring higher-order thinking skills as a means of improving the pupils' ability to predict;
- understand how the ICT curriculum can be enriched through 'learning to think' activities
- understand what prediction means;
- use prediction to investigate topics within the classroom setting;
- reflect on your own experiences of interpolation, extrapolation and pattern seeking;
- become a guide for pupils and develop their thinking skills, in particular those associated with analysis;
- help your pupils to become effective users of data.

OVERVIEW

Collecting large amounts of data, and processing it rapidly, are tasks that are well supported by the use of technology. Hypotheses and predictions can be developed quickly. The graph-plotting capability of spreadsheets allows pupils to look for patterns without having to re-plot the data manually. Modelling solutions and producing sophisticated simulations facilitates predictions. The technology is encouraging higher-order thinking skills as pupils can progress into analysis of the data rather than being limited to the tedium of collecting it.

Many studies have shown that teachers can affect the way in which their pupils' thinking develops. Adey and Shayer's work (1994) shows how teaching can become more effective through constructivist and metacognitive strategies. Although based in science education their work has many implications for ICT teaching. More recent studies have reported upon powerful pedagogic strategies. In particular, the work of Leat and Higgins has highlighted the value in exposing training teachers to teaching thinking and the role of 'powerful pedagogic strategies' (Leat, 1998). We will see how their use of 'mysteries' and 'living graphs' and the prediction activities can support learning in ICT.

Prediction links to the National Curriculum for England in several ways, including *Developing ideas and making things happen* (2b,2c) and *Reviewing, modifying and evaluating work as it progresses* (4c). At Key Stage 4 and post-16 education there are links to the testing aspects of the design cycle and then making proposals. A pupil proposal can be considered to be prediction because the pupil is 'predicting' that their proposal will be successful. Modelling and simulation, as well as monitoring and control, provide opportunities for prediction and the associated cognitive and strategic activities. Prediction relates to the selection of the correct ICT tool for the activity in hand and asking the right questions about a situation. There are elements of prediction relating to the implicit values – social, moral, ethical and political – that relate to the use of ICT and the personal philosophy of the value of ICT. An important element of the advanced use of ICT relates to planning, team management and ensuring that all eventualities are catered for in proposed solutions. Prediction also relates to probability and chance, and the skills of prediction relate to those of lateral thinking and the encouragement of pupils to be speculative. This is reflected in statements like 'reading between the lines', 'seeing the wood for the trees' and 'crystal-ball gazing'.

PATTERN SEEKING AND PREDICTING THROUGH GRAPHS

In this section we will see how the computer can be used to create lines and curves to help interpret data, interpolate and extrapolate, thus creating new data, and to speculate what future data may be. By structuring the learning environment we can ensure that the pupils consider what the probable results will be before testing and seeing. This will be illustrated by using graphing programs to develop mathematical skills and monitoring (sensing) programs supporting 'living graphs'.

CASE STUDY: FAMILIES OF CURVES

Families of curves show visual patterns, and missing elements can be predicted. The family $y = 2x + 6$, $y = 3x + 6$ and $y = 5x + 6$ can be used to help pupils understand the changes to the value m in the general expression for a graph $y = mx + c$. From the curves the shape of $y = 4x + 6$ can be interpolated (lying between the second and third) and by extrapolation the shapes of $y = 6x + 6$, $y = 7x + 6$ can be predicted. The pupils can then be challenged 'what do you think that $y = 100x + 6$ looks like? and $y = 0x + 6$? and $y = -3x + 6$?

COMMENTARY ON CASE STUDY

This same principle is then applied to more complex and challenging mathematical scenarios by mathematics colleagues. These include linear programming and breakeven-point analysis of the GCE specifications. Your use of a relevant application of modelling will motivate the pupils and move them on from the more trivial simulation examples.

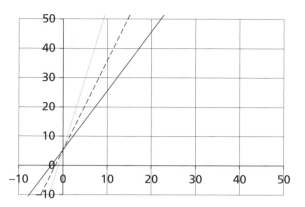

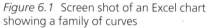
Figure 6.1 Screen shot of an Excel chart showing a family of curves

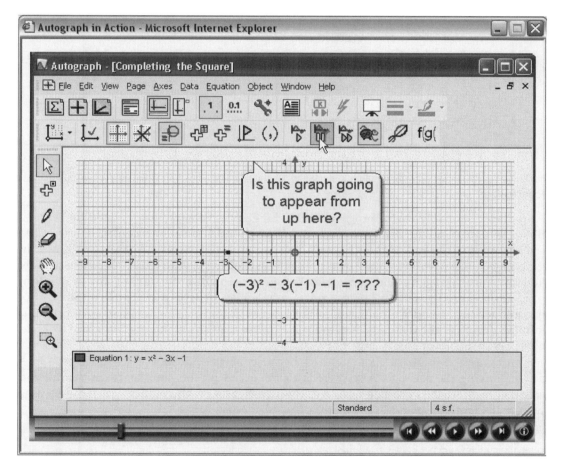

Figure 6.2 Screen shot of Autograph showing prediction

Activity 6.1   Graphing programs

Figure 6.1 was created using the Microsoft spreadsheet Excel. There are many graphing programs; some are suited to Key Stage 3 work and others to more advanced mathematical representations.

Activity 6.1 *continued*

1 Choose a graphing program or use the charting facilities of a spreadsheet to create images of curve families to stimulate discussion and prediction questions ('what do you think . . .') before giving pupils access to the programs to check their hypotheses.
2 Read about 'powerful pedagogic strategies'. Either search the internet or read Leat and Higgins (2002). They describe six characteristics of powerful pedagogic strategies. In what way do you consider using a charting program a good pedagogic method?

Which of the following apply to powerful pedagogic strategies?

- They represent a manageable unit of change.
- They are flexible.
- They set tasks with no single correct solution.
- They juxtapose the known with the new.
- They encourage talk.
- They are cross-subject.

Resources

Autograph is a really useful program with a range of 'screen movies' created by Douglas Butler to help the novice user learn the techniques of modelling with graphs. (For references, see Software at the end of this chapter.) The 'slow plot' feature of Autograph allows the graphing to be paused/resumed by tapping the spacebar. As Butler says, 'get them curious, and they are engaged'. One particular movie 'Completing the square' illustrates how prediction exercises can be carried out in whole-class teaching and how pupils can be encouraged to be cognitively engaged in the process. Coypu is a simpler program for plotting families of curves and data sets. A demonstration version is available for download from the Shell Centre at Nottingham University.

Omnigraph is highly recommended because of the additional teaching resources accompanying the package. Also there is a similarity with the popular Texas Instruments calculators. MathsNet provide resources for investigating mathematics which can be used with both Omnigraph and TI calculators.

Activity 6.2 Researching graphing programs

Use the internet to locate further information about graphing programs.

CASE STUDY: USING MONITORING SOFTWARE IN THE CLASSROOM

The pupils enter the classroom; the teacher gets their attention and says 'if we drew a graph of the sound level in this room throughout the lesson, what would it look like?'

A few suggestions are made and the teacher makes some informal sketches on the whiteboard and mentions x and y axes, units and timeline. The pupils are given a sheet of graph paper per group of four and asked to draw what they think will happen. These are called 'living graphs' (DfES, 2004d).

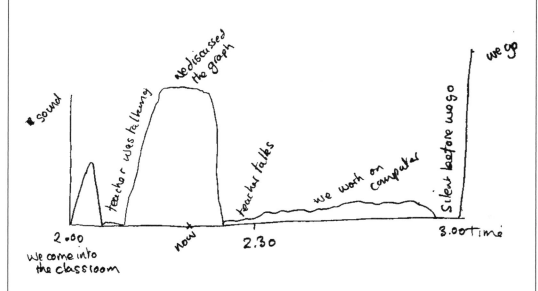

Figure 6.3 A living graph

The lesson continues, describing monitoring and control issues. Near the end of the lesson the teacher reveals the sound sensor readings and plot. The hypotheses drawn by the pupils are compared to the real events.

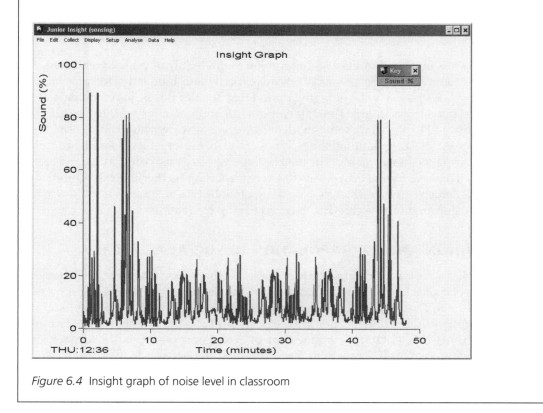

Figure 6.4 Insight graph of noise level in classroom

COMMENTARY ON THE CASE STUDY

Leoni Funfe, the teacher concerned, recommends that you 'set up such a scenario in a classroom if the school has a licence for data-logging software. All you need to do is link a sound sensor (microphone) to a computer hosting the data-logging program. Configure the software to pick up surrounding sound levels/intensity at a fixed or varying time interval and log them on the database. This data can then be plotted as a line graph for better interpretation. Higher set pupils will generally make sketches close to the real graph.'

In this situation the pupils have been asked to predict and record their predictions in the form of living graphs. They have been able to check their hypotheses against a reality that would be hard to detect without technology. The exercise gives them an understanding of the facilities and uses of monitoring hardware and software. It enables them to develop higher-order thinking skills.

Also, the activity places the learning in a context they are familiar with. When planning teaching activities you should endeavour to make the activity rich in curriculum content that places learning in a familiar context. The activities should develop learning skills and high-level thinking.

Activity 6.3 Contextualised learning

1   Use the internet to read about contextualised learning and in particular look for the work by Peter Jarvis (Jarvis, 2004).
2   The standard monitoring hardware kits have common sensors – nearly all have temperature probes, sound and light level sensors. Software usually found in schools provides the facility to log data over long periods of time. Set up the equipment to log light or temperature levels of the classroom over a 24-hour period. The output can be used by pupils to check their hypotheses.

Resources

Logotron Insight is impressive data-logging software with highly developed features set to strengthen the quality of Key Stage 3 and 4 Science experiments. Innovative features include a facility to display a powerful fast-logging option that enables pupils to record data at up to 100 samples per second in 'real time'. It comes with an interactive teaching guide. The Deltronics Sense and Control box comes with data logger software which can be used to set up experiments by selecting sampling rates, types of sensor (automatic sensor identification is supported), trigger conditions, etc. The data is displayed as a graph or graphs, and can be saved in its own internal format or exported to a spreadsheet for further analysis. Commotion produce LogIT which combines meters, a data logger, interface and analysis system in one portable unit using an intuitive green to start, red to stop navigation.

INTERPOLATION AND EXTRAPOLATION IN SOCIAL CONTEXTS

The social implication of the widespread use of ICT is an important element of the curriculum. An aim of the National Curriculum is that our best pupils can when 'discussing their own and others' use of ICT, use their knowledge and experience of information systems to inform their views on the social, economic, political, legal, ethical and moral issues' that are raised by the use of ICT (DfEE, 1999). This is a measure of exceptional performance but each level of the attainment target for ICT capability has a stepping stone to this highest level.

Interpolation can be considered, in this context, to be the art of reading between the lines and of speculation about a situation which then leads to justification for those assertions.

This activity is prone to prejudice and problems associated with blinkered thinking or narrow-mindedness. Past experience and reflections upon previous judgements play an important role in this area.

Extrapolation is examining the scenarios and considering the possible outcomes. It is making hypotheses or predicting the future. In social contexts a person's ideas about the future will be impacted upon by their more recent experiences. In this area of considering the role and values of ICT we are trying to broaden the pupils' experience and understanding and by so doing broaden their expectations.

We will look at two scenarios. The first has been used successfully in classrooms for over ten years. The scenario remains the same, but the outcomes have changed in the light of the ever-developing technologies and the more pervasive nature of ICT at work, in the home and in leisure activities.

CASE STUDY: EXPLORATION ACTIVITY 1

A park ranger (David) has recently retired from work at an English Nature SSI in the Beacon Hills at the age of 58. Now at home all day, hobbies and interests are important to him. His elderly mother (Catherine), who suffers from a heart condition, lives 10 miles away in a small village. His grandchildren (Mattie and Becky) attend Swanborough School and have access to a range of computers; they also have a computer at home.

- Describe a medical technique that uses an electronic device that will make Catherine's health more secure.

  _____

- Describe a device that Catherine could have in her home that would mean she could call for help most easily, and describe a device that would automatically call for help if Catherine did not get up on a particular morning.

  _____

- There is no bank or post office in the village where David lives. Describe an information service and a banking service that David could use from his home.

  _____

- Describe how David and his grandchildren could use the internet to keep in touch with each other, and describe how his grandchildren use information technology in their work at school.

  _____

COMMENTARY ON EXPLORATION ACTIVITY 1

These notes are useful starting points for discussions and factual lessons. Through them we can contextualise their learning. Pupils need to be able to discuss the social, economic, ethical and moral aspects of information technology. That discussion should be based upon a wide experience and knowledge of information and communication systems. These discussions can be placed in core ICT lessons or PSHE sessions. The pupils are using skills of interpolation and extrapolation. They need to make some assumptions when recommending or suggesting ICT solutions. It is exercises like these that get the children thinking about the subject instead of simply seeking the right answer in simple multiple-choice questions.

CASE STUDY: EXPLORATION ACTIVITY 2

In this second scenario, the information given is not so explicit. A greater degree of interpolation, or reading between the lines, is required. There are also a number of 'red herrings' which lead to an interest and engagement in the material. And an important difference is that the questions are not as focused. This exercise is less suitable for homework or individual study, but benefits from discussion.

Put each of these items of information on separate cards. Give one set to each group of pupils. Ask them to sort the cards. After a few moments give them the questions to focus upon. You will need to provide information about current computers and peripherals, preferably in a computer catalogue:

Stella has a flip-phone.
After putting the children to bed Stella relaxes by reading a book.
On her birthday, Stella went to a singles bar with her mate.
Stella works in a shop.
Stella likes cooking.
Stella was born in Birmingham and went to college in London.
Stella's car is an Audi A6.
Stella's boss is often away from work travelling on business.
There is a parents' evening on Wednesday.
Stella voted for Labour last month.
Stella's favourite colour is purple and her favourite food is chocolate mousse.
Stella's neighbour has a boat.
Stella's mum has two married sons.
Stella is 1.6m tall, weighs 71 kg and has size 38 shoes.

Using this information and the computer catalogue, explain why Stella will pay £1,100 for her first computer and peripherals, and explain what she will do with it.

COMMENTARY ON EXPLORATION ACTIVITY 2

The Stella exercise is described as a 'mystery'. Further examples can be found in *Leading in Learning: Exemplification in ICT* (DfES, 2004f). It is an example of a 'powerful pedagogic strategy'. It is a device whereby we can get pupils to really think about the issue and actively engage with the material. Importantly, these activities lend themselves to small group work and the subsequent learning we recognise as socially constructed.

Activity 6.4 Mysteries and constructivism

1   Read about 'mysteries' and their use. Devise a mystery exercise that relates specifically to the people, events or places associated with your school or your pupils.
2   Create a grid with your mystery statements and print it on card. Place the cut cards into an envelope and distribute one envelope to each group of pupils. If pupils are familiar with the 'mystery' technique then a way of differentiating the activity is to ask a more able group to devise their own mystery or modify the cards of the mystery you have given.

Activity 6.4 *continued*

3   Read about constructivism. A useful summary can be found in *Learning and Teaching in Secondary Schools* (Kinchin, 2002: 24–26) and a more extensive discussion by Leask and Younie (2001: 117–133). Alternatively, carry out a search on the internet. My recommended source for information on learning theory is *Funderstanding* (see Websites at the end of this chapter).

USING MODELS AND SIMULATIONS TO PREDICT OUTCOMES OF CHANGES

Models and simulations have been popular since the earliest stages of educational computing. Simple graphic character representation of two canal lock gates and water levels enabled pupils to create a 'program' of step-by-step instructions to make a boat ascend from the lower level to the higher level. Adventure games like Granny's Garden introduced decision-making and exploration. In both cases it was possible to enter instructions that did not necessarily give the correct answer. The boat did not ascend or the children got caught by the wicked witch. Being able to do more than the single option is the essence of exploration. It is the way in which computers can give a range of choices for pupils to pursue.

Prediction needs more. Prediction needs the learner to articulate the reasoning for the choice, based upon the information given. Prediction is a higher-order skill.

Models are simulations that can be changed. In models the variables and conditions within the simulation are under the control of the user, and this gives a greater opportunity for more sophisticated exploration. We will consider one particular model used to teach the subject knowledge and understanding within geography at advanced level, but first consider the value of using models in teaching. In a recent review of the educational literature of ICT-rich learning environments, the new paradigms of Science teaching were examined: promoting cognitive change, formative assessment and lifelong learning in the context of the use of ICT and models in particular (Webb, 2005). Models are important because they:

*   can help visualise or experience scenarios that learners cannot experience for real because they are too dangerous, time-consuming or expensive;
*   can be the basis for the learners to understand theory by integrating discrete items of knowledge;
*   can increase learners' motivation and interest in the subject matter and thus increase cognitive engagement.

Importantly for ICT teachers, the use of spreadsheet, multimedia or script-based models increases the understanding of the value of the generic software.

Using models enables learners to learn from making good decisions. They can also learn from making bad decisions; something that might be too emotionally or professionally costly in the real world. The advantage of learning to make predictions through simulations is that the consequences of poor decision-making are virtually cost-free yet have value in 'learning from mistakes'. The prediction cycle is reflected in Figure 6.5, which shows a diagrammatic representation of a model.

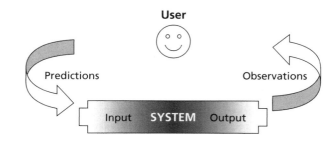

Figure 6.5 Prediction cycle

CASE STUDY: MODELLING ACTIVITY

Hydrograph is one of a series of models developed at Peter Symonds College, Winchester as part of a project to make independent learning more effective. The curriculum content is GCE-level Geography but the principles of learning through models can be applied to many areas of the curriculum. The aim of the interactive presentation is to help pupils understand: what factors influence a river's flood behaviour; why different rivers have different flood risks; how we can predict flood risk by studying the river; and how sample flood events have influenced people. The pupils are taken through a series of activities which isolate each of the factors that influence flooding. By moving a slide bar they can see the impact of changing the single variable. Each variable is identified, introduced and explored in turn.

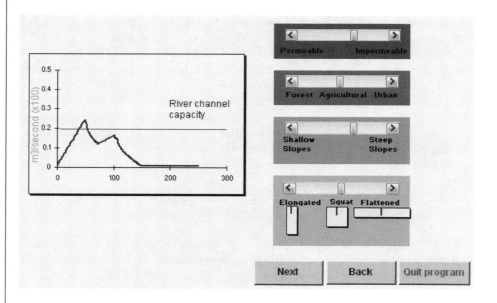

Figure 6.6 Hydrograph

The final activity combines the facility to change all variables independently of each other. The pupils are guided: 'On the model above, an imaginary river channel has a capacity of 20 cubic metres per second (as shown on the red line). If the water level exceeds this line, a flood will occur. Using the four variables on the slider bars, construct five or six descriptions of different drainage basins. . . . Use the slider bars to investigate each basin you describe. Sketch the graph and explain whether or not that particular basin would be prone to flooding.'

COMMENTARY ON MODELLING ACTIVITY

The importance of this model in the curriculum is both to motivate the pupils and to enable them to become engaged in the subject matter. The activities involve discussion and decision-making. The pupils can also learn through reinforcement. They can carry out their own predictions outside of the lesson. The activity supports independent learning. 'Like other models we use, Hydrograph interests the pupils. . . . they are able to see the impact of change. . . . our curriculum is about understanding the influence that we are having on the environment.' (Moya Grove, geography teacher). When explaining the industrial and commercial role of modelling and simulations and before introducing the technicalities of a spreadsheet-based activity it is always motivating to show the pupils working, sophisticated models.

Activity 6.5 Prediction in practice

1   Consider the questions and instructions you would use to encourage prediction. How will you set up the learning activity?

_____

_____

_____

2   How would you explain that they should not simply type in a number to get the answer but to write down the number, write down what answer or perhaps possible answers the computer model might give, write down the reasons. Then check by entering the number and seeing the answer. It is then important to explain if the model gave an unexpected result.

_____

_____

_____

3   The focus may be a database search using AND, OR or NOT. Given the query, the pupils should first be asked to predict what the result will be with an explanation, then try to explain if the result was unexpected. Before making an internet search, consider what the results might be. For example, using Google, what might the result of these two searches be:

   • Control OR CPU
   • Control AND CPU?

_____

_____

_____

Write down your plans in terms of what you would like to see the pupils doing and what they are supposed to be learning. Be clear that your description clearly explains to the pupils why they are doing the exercise.

_____

_____

_____

_____

_____

Resources

The following resources all offer the opportunity to create prediction activities. Flowol from Data Harvest enables pupils to create control programs. Like playing chess, there are a limited number of simple rules but a world of strategies that can be developed. Flowol supports sub-routines, multi-tasking, variables and feedback from both digital and analogue inputs to start and stop events.

Fairground ride simulation from Funderstanding needs a java-enabled browser to run the coaster applet. Pupils are responsible for setting the controls for the height of the different hills, the size of the loop, the initial speed of the coaster, its mass, the gravity at work and the amount of friction on the track.

Another Roller Coaster simulation is from the science section of the University of Cambridge's Brainteasers and Puzzles website. 'You need to find the perfect combination . . . just enough thrills to keep the customers excited but not so bumpy that they throw up or faint!'

Mangodata from Sherston Software is a multi-user database that allows pupils to easily enter information and then search the data to display results through a range of graphs and charts. This information might include a class survey, historical census information, or perhaps the results of scientific investigations. The multi-user feature allows different pupils to enter data into the same database at the same time – pupils can access a database from the same network, from different schools, or even from different countries!

Biz Wiz from 4Mation software is a small business simulator used to computer concepts, commerce, business studies and computing studies. Pupils can interact with the bank, use an employment agency and a market analyst, hire and fire staff, advertise and purchase parts. They will also have to set a keen market price for their products to ensure they remain competitive in the computer market (see also Chapter 8 concerning this type of simulation).

Discussion

In this chapter we have seen that simulations can be the focus of prediction activities. Simulations are also motivating and encourage cognitive engagement. An important motivation driver of simulations is the immediacy of their response to learner input, but to make the prediction activity more effective we have to slow down the learner activity to ensure that they make considered and rationalised decisions. We must keep a careful balance between these two factors to avoid losing the motivational aspect of simulations.

Prediction requires the learner to exercise self-discipline. It requires us to structure the learning resources and our instructions to the pupils to ensure that the learners gain from the experience. It is important that we are clear about the reasons for carrying out the activity and ensure that the learners understand the rationale for predicting. By describing our lessons in terms of what we are expecting the pupils to learn and what we will expect to see them doing we will create a more effective learning environment.

A capability that pupils need to develop their skills of prediction includes visual literacy. Visual literacy is the ability, through knowledge of the basic visual elements, to understand the meaning and components of the image whether it is a chart, graph, picture, icon, animation or movie. In other areas the verbal literacy skills of the pupils are challenged. Text-based and spoken vignettes are common in everyday life and schooling in general. Pupils in ICT lessons can use their skills to better understand the concepts of ICT, especially those associated with ethical, moral, social and economic issues.

The skills of prediction also require self-discipline from learners so that they don't just jump to find the answer, but make a guess first and rationalise their assertions before checking their hypotheses. The affordances of the computer to enable the development of these higher-order thinking skills are: the speed of response, the numerical representation of concepts (gradient, intersect points, average and trend), the visualisation of concepts (narrow channel, broad basin, flash flood), the ability to 'undo' actions so that other decisions can be made, and the facility to repeat activities.

We can help pupils to predict through targeted activities and by giving a clear indication that it is the process that is more important than the product or answer. When introducing the ICT lessons, we use phrases such as 'We Are Learning To' (WALT, see Chapter 3) gain the skills of prediction, to make better guesses or to discover new facts from the data. It is important that we introduce the concept of self-discipline and ask the pupils to hold back from finding the answers. We need to articulate that 'What I'm Looking For' (WILF) is the pupil making predictions, using good guessing based upon past experience, and discovering new facts. The pupils also need to understand that 'This Is Because' (TIB) in life we need to be able to predict what might happen in any situation if we are to make the best decisions.

SUMMARY

In this chapter we have seen some ways in which you can use ICT in the classroom to support hypotheses and prediction and how modern technology is enabling pattern seeking, extrapolation and interpolation to help learners analyse and understand data. Pattern is repetition and prediction is recognising the patterns that exist in data. Through the use of ICT learners can identify trends in values. Pupils can make sense and draw information from a mass of data by systematically applying strategies.

FURTHER READING

DfES (2004) *Leading in Learning: Developing Thinking Skills at Key Stage 3* London: DfES.

WEBSITES

Funderstanding: www.funderstanding.com.

SOFTWARE

Autograph: www.autograph-maths.com/inaction
Coypu: www.nottingham.ac.uk/education/shell/
Omnigraph: www.spasoft.co.uk
MathsNet: www.mathsnet.net/omnigraph.html
Insight: www.logo.com
Sense and Control box: www.deltronics.co.uk
LogIT: www.commotiongroup.co.uk
Flowol: www.data-harvest.co.uk/control/flo_software.html
Rollercoaster: http://www.funderstanding.com/k12/coaster
Cambridge University Brainteasers and Puzzles: http://puzzling.caret.cam.ac.uk
Mangodata: www2.sherston.com
Bizwiz: www.4mation.co.uk/cat/bizwiz.html.

Chapter 7   Communication

MARTYN LAWSON

INTRODUCTION

In this chapter we will look at the ways in which you can use ICT in the classroom to support communication, and how modern technology is changing the nature of communication in the twenty-first century. In particular, we will attempt to answer the following questions:

- How can we use communication activities in the classroom?
- What capabilities will we need to communicate effectively?
- What does technology bring to the communicating process in the twenty-first century?
- How can we develop our pupils' ability to communicate through targeted activities in school?

By the end of this chapter you should be able to:

- see the potential for using more adventurous and interesting communication-based activities with your pupils as a means of improving their ability to communicate and also as a way of enlivening the ICT curriculum.

HOW CAN WE USE COMMUNICATION ACTIVITIES IN THE CLASSROOM?

Whenever we turn to discussion of the 'C' in ICT, we inevitably become engaged in a consideration of children's literacy, and, by virtue of the use of a keyboard as an input device, very often consideration of their ability to write. Traditional input methods for ICT devices result largely in written forms of communication, and even today in the environment of voice-driven input devices, the majority of interaction with computers still consists of input via a keyboard of some kind.

> Prospective employers, examiners and the general public see the art of writing as the most fundamental test of a person's ability to communicate clearly and accurately.
>
> (Sargeant, 1995)

You will most likely be aware that written communication is something that many children experience difficulties with. Many do not like writing, and underperform when comparing their written abilities with their overall level of potential. For example: 'attainment in writing is still too low and lags far behind attainment in reading' (Ofsted, 2004: 9) and 'The performance of boys, particularly in writing, has lagged behind that of girls for a long time' (Ofsted, 2004: 8).

You will also be conscious of the requirement placed upon you as a teacher to actively plan for the improvement of your pupils' literacy in your lessons (whatever subject you are teaching) (DfES, 2002: 11). Yet the process of writing goes beyond the production of com--munication in written form:

> Whenever writing takes place there is always a purpose and an intended reader. Sometimes we write for ourselves and in this case:

- Writing helps in the capture and development of thoughts and ideas, because it leaves a record that can be returned to, considered and modified.

> At other times, we write with the intention of communicating to others, which contributes to learning because:

- Communicating in writing clarifies, confirms, even transforms understanding through a complex process of:

  - Linking ideas and pieces of information and organising them logically;
  - 'wrestling' with words to form clear, meaningful sentences.

> DfES (2004g: 8)

Furthermore, according to Sewell:

> We thus have a perspective which envisages writing as being a tool in the development of metacognition. When children reflect on the nature of their writing, they are, in essence, utilizing a metacognitive skill – they are thinking about the implications of their own thinking. In dealing with writing, children have to distinguish between what is intended and what is actually expressed in the written message.

> (1990: 172)

Hence the process of writing is vitally important in the development of the critical reasoning and reflective abilities of the child. Writing develops cognitive skills.

Of course, literacy, and particularly literacy that is facilitated by technology, does not just confine itself to writing, but it is important to distinguish between transient and non-transient types of communication. We can classify writing as a non-transient form of communication – it is one that allows reflection and revision, whereas speech is more often transient – what is said cannot be retracted or easily revised. So, even when exploiting communication technologies such as digital video, email, speech recognition, voice over IP, most of the technology-supported communications either are or can be recorded and thus are non-transient (the only one in the above list that is likely to be transient is 'voice over IP', although that could be recorded if required). Hence, the technologies that are most usually available to us in the classroom (and the technologies that are emerging) create non-transient communication. Consequently we can use these technologies to help our pupils develop their cognitive skills just as much as if they were writing a report or essay. In fact, in most cases it will be easier, because the nature of the activities we can use with the support of technology is likely to be more engaging for many pupils than the prospect of some kind of traditional writing activity.

The emergence of networked technologies over the past decade or so, for example in the form of the internet, email and mobile telephones, has fundamentally changed the nature of communication. It is now possible, using these technologies to communicate across greater geographic (and cultural) distances, more or less instantaneously and sometimes to a large audience many of whom you do not know, nor will ever meet. In 1997, the government's consultation paper over the proposed National Grid for Learning, identified networked literacy as being:

> the capacity to use electronic networks to access resources, to create resources, and to communicate with others. These elements of network literacy can be seen as extensions of the traditional skills of reading, writing, speaking and listening.
>
> (DfEE, 1997: 10)

Whilst there are some challenges associated with this, there are also many opportunities. It is important that we equip our pupils with the skills and knowledge that they need to exploit these opportunities whilst at the same time making them conscious of the challenges.

This chapter provides some ideas about how technology can be used at both the input and output stage of the communication process. It also illustrates in a practical way how classroom activities can utilise technology as a way of developing communication skills in your pupils.

For example, newsroom simulations were popular classroom activities some years ago in a number of areas of the curriculum. In recent years they have been less commonly used, but the current technology of ICT does allow us to look again at such simulations as a tool for communicating. Appendix C gives a sequence of fictitious reports relating to a helicopter crash which actually took place in the 1980s in the Lake District.

The serial reports indicate a developing emergence of news and detail about the event. They are intended to provide a story that could be used as a 'newsroom' or 'reportage' simulation. For example, the idea below focuses on timeliness and immediacy in communication and how ICT can be used to support the production and dissemination of timely information to a wide audience. Potential learning objectives for this could include:

- Report news in succinct form.
- Work against a deadline.
- Recognise that not all information they will need is available at the same time.
- Be selective about the detail they include in their report.
- Consider the potential audience for their communication and adjust the content accordingly.
- Recognise the importance of timeliness of communication even if this is at the expense of detail and accuracy.

Activity 7.1 Newsroom simulation

1   Plan an ICT lesson and gather appropriate resources to use the idea above with a class of fifteen-year-olds that you teach.
2   Try it out and then evaluate its usefulness and success.
3   Consider what makes this ICT lesson different from a similar activity carried out in an English lesson.

This activity can contribute to learning objectives in both ICT and English. The focus of the teaching and the reflective plenary will vary according to the subject setting.

WHAT CAPABILITIES WILL WE NEED TO COMMUNICATE EFFECTIVELY?

Capabilities in this context usually mean some kind of formal process that the pupil undertakes. For communication to be really effective it has to be planned in advance and the ideas developed in a rigorous and systematic way. Some people have the tremendous knack of producing spontaneous, high-quality communication, but not many of your pupils will be able to do this with consistency and across a range of genres or media. Also, even those people who seem to be able to communicate really effectively with little effort or obvious planning are probably well rehearsed in their craft and have honed their skill with lots of practice. Hence there is some importance in devoting time to the development of a selection of core capabilities. Consideration of these issues will mean that your pupils are more likely to at least think about the communication they are involved in. The activities in this section provide some ideas about how to engage with these core capabilities in the classroom.

Making sense and meaning

Central to the process of communication are the skills of reading, writing, speaking and listening. There are many texts elsewhere (Gamble and Easingwold (2000) for example) that can help you to understand some of the ways in which children develop these skills, and this chapter is not intended to cover these fundamental communication skills in detail. However, all of these core skills have a role to play in making sense and meaning of communication. In order for communication to be effective it must be understood and our minds have a tremendous ability to try and create meaning (sometimes even where no meaning exists). If you consider the poem 'Jaberwocky' by Lewis Carrol, many of the words themselves have no meaning, yet when we read it or hear it read to us, we create a meaning for the nonsense words. However, sometimes we get meanings wrong – even with words and sentences that appear to make sense. An example of this is illustrated by the game of 'Chinese Whispers' where a message changes as it passes from person to person until the final message bears little resemblance to the original.

In other communication media, this making sense of meaning happens as well. Slang expressions are often created from words that have no meaning, yet they create a meaning by their use in context. Also in some cases the meaning of words is changed by the means of common usage. English is full of words that have changed their meaning over time. The word 'awful' for example originally meant full of awe, yet nowadays we use it to mean terrible or of poor quality. You may have seen the text below in a number of places on the internet (for one example, see Websites at the end of this chapter).

THE PAOMNNEHAL PWEOR OF THE HMUAN MNID

Aoccdrnig to a rscheearch at Cmabrigde Uinervtisy, it deosn't mttaer In waht oredr the ltteers in a wrod are, the olny iprmoatnt tihng is that the frist and lsat ltteer be in the rghit pclae. The rset can be a taotl mses and you can sitll raed it wouthit porbelm.

Tihs is bcuseae the huamn mnid deos not raed ervey lteter by istlef, but the wrod as a wlohe.

Amzanig huh? Cdnuolt blveiee taht I cluod aulaclty uesdnatnrd waht I was rdgnieg.

In a similar way, visual representations also cause us to infer meaning. Every time you look at a famous logo your mind creates the connection between the logo and the brand. The KS3 ICT strategy has some useful material relating to graphical logos in sample teaching unit 7.3 (DfES, 2002) that would be worth looking at again in the light of this discussion. Matthewman and Trigg (2004) describe some classroom-based research that looks at the use of font selection and appropriate images as a means of adding meaning to written text. However, again, this visual representation can also be fooled or confused. There is a famous experiment in psychology called the Stroop experiment (see Websites at the end of this chapter). In this experiment, the subject is shown a series of colour names – red, blue, green, and so on – in quick succession and asked to repeat the name they are reading. The words are coloured in the same colour as the colour represented by the name, so for example the word red is in red text. After the series has been running for a time, some 'rogue' name and colour combinations are unexpectedly shown, so for example the name red is shown in blue text. When this happens, the subject often stumbles or reads the name incorrectly. There is dissonance between the name and the colour and the brain has trouble in making sense of this dissonance.

A really valuable effect of association of images with words can be found in a number of educational settings. For example, people who have difficulty communicating through traditional spoken or written forms may be able to associate pictures or sounds with words. There is some excellent software available to assist very young children and also children with SEN that utilises this ability of the brain to connect symbols, pictures, sounds and words together and hence enables people to communicate where otherwise they would be unable to.

Other capabilities can be seen to be more practical and technical. They include:

Drafting

Drafting is the process of producing the original ideas in some form (usually written) so that further refinement and development can take place before the final version is produced.

Re-drafting

The further refinement and development referred to above is re-drafting.

Editing

Very often, editing involves what literacy specialists call 'word-level' work. Your pupils will probably be familiar with spell-checking and perhaps even checking grammar and proofreading their work, and these skills are integral to the editing process. However, editing can also include shortening a longer piece of work or perhaps rewriting parts of the text in order to improve it or tailor it for a particular purpose or audience.

Audience

Most forms of communication produced in the classroom need to be considered in terms of audience. In ICT, your pupils are likely to be familiar with this concept, as sense of audience plays a major part of the work done in the early Year 7 units in the ICT KS3 strategy. However, the points made in those units are no less important here.

CASE STUDY: WRITING FRAME FOR A LEVEL ICT

GCE ICT involves a considerable amount of project work. The final product of this work is a written report which is marked according to a set of criteria established by the examination board. Many post-16 students have real difficulties in writing these reports and consequently do not do themselves justice in their marks. Working on the principle that it is always easier to start from something rather than a blank screen or piece of paper, Sue Wood, a teacher of ICT at A level, has devised a template (or writing frame) that is used in the Outline feature of Word. The students are presented with this outline and expected to develop content to fill in the detail between each heading in the outliner. This provides a structure for the student which is non-negotiable. The student can see exactly what elements are required to produce a report in the appropriate format.

COMMENTARY ON CASE STUDY

One benefit of a template such as this is that the template expands as the detailed text is added. It is a growing and developing thing rather than just a list of headings presented on a separate piece of paper. Also, being an outline, it is possible for the pupil to start with the basic list, add some points at the next level and then organise their thoughts and ideas, allowing the possibility of revision and redrafting of sections.

Activity 7.2   Help with the written report

1   What style should a written report of this nature be in?

2   How could you help your pupils to become aware of this style and comfortable in using it?

3   How could you use examples of previously produced project work to assist your pupils?

Here are some suggested responses:

- An analysis of existing scripts, either published by the examination boards or generated by previous pupils, could be used to devise a collection of successful stylistic examples.
- You could produce some models of good stylistic practice – for example opening sentences for each section of the report.
- You could encourage your pupils to take responsibility for peer evaluation of each others' work.

Activity 7.3   Current and future practice

1   Reflect on your current practice in relation to the support you give to the writing of coursework reports.
2   Plan the support you will give to your pupils in the future.

WHAT DOES TECHNOLOGY BRING TO THE COMMUNICATING PROCESS IN THE TWENTY-FIRST CENTURY?

Spontaneity

Notwithstanding what has been said elsewhere in this chapter, modern communication technologies allow us the opportunity to communicate in more obviously spontaneous ways. For instance, email and text messaging have, to a large extent, engaged what would be otherwise reluctant writers in written forms of communication that are immediate and have many of the characteristics of colloquial spoken communication. Formal conventions of written English are often disregarded as the technology is encouraging speed of response, economy of writing (typing) effort and volume of interaction. David Lodge in his novel *Thinks* provides some useful advice:

> you're going to have to loosen up your prose style for email. speed is the essence for instance dont bother with caps because they take up time unnecessarily, two key strokes instead of one and dont bother with correcting typos.
>
> (Lodge, 2002: 184)

Lynne Truss (2003) in her book *Eats, Shoots & Leaves* has some further thoughts on the subject:

> This is an exciting time for the written word: it is adapting to the ascendant medium, which happens to be the most immediate, universal and democratic written medium that has ever existed.
>
> (Truss, 2003: 180)

Originally recognised as a feature of email correspondence, informality of communication has in recent years, and by many school-aged children and young people, been adopted far more readily for the purpose of text messaging using mobile telephones. To some extent, what is emerging is almost a new language where abbreviations, phonic substitutions and numbers masquerading as words are freely used to convey a message in the shortest time and number of keystrokes as possible. Hence a message such as 'cu @ 8?', meaning 'Shall I see you at 8 o'clock?', asks a question using only eleven key presses (including spaces), thus saving nineteen key presses from the full, conventional written question (assuming predictive text completion is not used). According to Grinter and Eldridge (2001), text messaging is changing the way in which (predominantly) young people communicate with each other. They identify four main reasons for teenagers to use text messaging:

- making arrangements;
- coordinating with friends (often through synchronous communication – known as hypercoordinating);
- chatting and gossiping;
- coordinating with family (also includes hypercoordinating).

(Grinter and Eldridge, 2001: 227–228)

Of course there are pitfalls with writing in this abbreviated form, and the stylistic conventions of email writing have been well documented (for example, by Netiquette, 2005). Also, we need to remember that effective texting is not the same as effective literacy! However, it is important not to lose sight of the fact that even in its abbreviated form, communication is taking place, using and facilitated by modern technology. In an environment where there are many difficulties in trying to persuade children and young people to write anything, here is an opportunity to exploit a medium with which most of our pupils are very comfortable. The added benefit is that is gives us a chance to explore the technology that supports their communication in new and potentially interesting ways.

CASE STUDY: USING 'TEXT SPEAK'

A teacher of KS3 ICT was using the ICT strategy material in unit 7.1 (DfES, 2002) with her Year 7 class. However, she allowed the children to use 'text speak' in their presentations about themselves. Then, when the children made their presentations to the class, they were required to check that the rest of the class understood the symbols or abbreviations that they had used on each slide.

This process raised some really interesting and contentious discussion amongst the class about meanings, accessibility and use of language. It also allowed the teacher to initiate a discussion about why 'text speak' was a medium that the children wanted to use and some of the difficulties that can be caused by its use.

Activity 7.4 Substitutes for words

Consider the material in the KS3 strategy, unit 7.3 (DfES, 2002). This unit is about producing a newsletter and incorporating appropriate images in a document. You might like to think about how you could engage your class in consideration of different ways of communicating the message. You might consider:

- incorporating images into text as substitutes for words;
- using abbreviations or symbols instead of words (look at examples of common commercial logos and URLs);
- how the audience will influence the choice of medium.

HOW CAN WE DEVELOP OUR PUPILS' ABILITY TO COMMUNICATE THROUGH TARGETED ACTIVITIES IN SCHOOL?

The examples above have tended to focus on written communication, but current technology provides many possibilities for communication using different media and in contexts that might otherwise be very difficult, if not impossible.

For example, a recent article (Williams, 2005) describes the use of video-conferencing in Holy Cross School in New Malden, Surrey. This provides a very useful overview of how video-conferencing can be used in the school to support creativity in the curriculum across international, multicultural boundaries.

Activity 7.5 Video-conferencing

1   The emergence of inexpensive webcam and headset hardware, coupled with software solutions using the internet that in some cases are free to use, allows the use of low-resolution video-conferencing without the need for expensive bespoke solutions. Consider how you might incorporate this technology into the curriculum.

2   Note that there is a discipline associated with successful use of video-conferencing technology. It would be interesting to get your pupils to produce a list of do's and don'ts based on their experience of trying the technology in class.

Discussion of responses

There are disciplines involved in communicating, whatever the medium, but spoken communication when it is in the form of a conversation is a particularly good example. For example: taking turns, not 'hogging' the conversation, listening skills, cue recognition, relevance of comment, and so on. Sometimes young people have difficulty in recognising and applying some of these disciplines, so an exercise where they collectively identify the often non-verbal signals that mediate spoken communication can be a very powerful way of highlighting the social conventions that allow successful conversation to happen.

Activity 7.6   Wikis and blogs

Find out about 'wikis' and 'blogs' (see Websites at the end of this chapter for definitions if you do not know what they are already). Look at the potential uses of them in your classroom. Some of these activities will need to be well moderated (particularly if the children are using blogs hosted outside the school), but these types of communication media allow some of the spontaneity of text messaging, only with a wider audience.

Activity 7.7   Final reflection

There are many opportunities in our curriculum for developing the communication skills of our pupils. Having read this chapter, reflect on your teaching and consider how the activities that you use in the classroom engage your pupils in communicating. Also look carefully at the tasks you set (wherever they have come from) and think about how you could use technology to vary, support and enliven the communication that is happening within the tasks and the classroom.

Share your ideas and activities with colleagues. Use ideas and amend them to suit your context. Despite what is often thought, teenagers can be enthusiastic communicators, provided that we ensure that both the medium and the message are interesting and stimulating to them.

SUMMARY

Communicating, whether through presenting to an audience, producing a publication, or sending messages over a distance, is the most common application of ICT, and the one with the most frequent use in other areas of the curriculum. As a result, it can become familiar and repetitive. This chapter has explored some new technologies – and new approaches to using familiar ones – which can invigorate the teaching of this area of the ICT curriculum.

FURTHER READING

Gamble, N. and Easingwood, N. (2000) *ICT and Literacy: Information and Communications Technology, Media, Reading and Writing*, London: Continuum.

Matthewman, S. and Triggs, P. (2004) 'Obsessive compulsive font disorder: the challenge of supporting pupils writing with the computer', *Computers and Education* 43: 125–135.

Lodge, D. (2002) *Thinks*, London: Penguin Books.

Sewell. D.F. (1990) *New Tools for New Minds*, New York: Harvester Wheatsheaf.

WEBSITES

Reading exercise: mailman.anu.edu.au/pipermail/link/2004-May/056713.html

Stroop experiments: faculty.washington.edu/chudler/words.html

Definitions: www.whatis.techtarget.com.

Chapter 8   Exploration

LYNNE DAGG

INTRODUCTION

In this chapter we will look at the ways in which you can use ICT in the classroom to support pupils in exploring information. In particular, we will attempt to answer the following questions:

- How can we use exploration in the classroom?
- What capabilities will we need to explore effectively?
- What does technology bring to the concept of exploring?
- How can we develop our pupils' ability to explore through targeted activities in school?

By the end of this chapter you should be able to:

- understand what exploration means and how to avoid getting lost!
- use exploration to investigate topics within the classroom setting;
- reflect on your own experiences as an explorer;
- become a guide for pupils (being aware of their need for safety and the danger of information overload);
- help your pupils to become effective explorers.

INTERPRETATIONS OF EXPLORATION

What do we mean by 'exploration'? It does not mean 'wander aimlessly around a website in the hope that you will remember some unspecified part of it at some future time'. That isn't exploration. It is a recipe for wasting valuable teaching and learning time.

The use of exploration as a teaching technique is not new (Scriven, 1970), nor is the idea of letting the pupils 'discover by themselves as much as is feasible under the given circumstances' (Polya, 1963) – the latter can be viewed as being exploration.

Exploration is 'the act of searching or travelling for the purpose of discovery' (Wikipedia, 2005a). For the purpose of this chapter, exploration is a technique that allows the pupil to investigate something with the objective of discovery. It is important that we know what pupils need to discover (i.e., the objective of the exploration) yet also provide opportunities to allow pupils to find out more than the minimum they need. We need to allow greater freedom for pupils as their exploration and information skills improve.

Writers such as de Bono have suggested that exploration needs no such constraints – 'You simply want to explore an area. You do not have a purpose other than to find out more about the area' (de Bono,1996). But de Bono was considering the use of exploration as a thinking purpose rather than as an activity for pupils. 'An explorer who lands on the moon or explores a remote part of Papua New Guinea has the purpose of finding out more' (de Bono, 1996). An explorer brings with them a set of expectations and previous experiences that will shape the exploration – a volcanologist is unlikely to explore the behaviour of individuals in the locality but will be likely to explore any volcanos or rocks they find. In fact the great explorers had a motive for their discovery. Colombus's exploration aimed to find the way to India from the West – even if the result was that he found the West Indies. For James Cook, it was a search for a mythical continent of 'Terra Australia' that led him to discover New Zealand and Australia's east coast. At heart, most exploring has a purpose – although it is acknowledged that this may not be the outcome of the exploration.

HOW CAN WE USE EXPLORATION IN THE CLASSROOM?

It is important to help our pupils to explore because they are young and inexperienced, although we would hope that they would eventually become independent explorers. We need to guide them into the process of exploring and keep them from danger, although as their exploring skills and their awareness of dangers increase, the less guidance they will need. Let us assume we took eleven-year-olds to an unfamiliar forest some miles from school and told them to explore it and that we would meet them back at school. We would, as educators, be acting recklessly. Would the pupils have an adventure? Yes. Would we get them all back to school? Possibly. Would they really explore the forest or would they spend their time trying to find the route back to school? When we take young people to a forest, we would know what we want them to learn from the experience (i.e., the learning objective). It could be that we want them to learn to map-read and we will provide them with maps and compasses and a route for them to follow. We probably would ensure that they had sufficent provisions to prevent them becoming dehydrated. We would also probably meet them at points in the forest to make sure that they didn't go too far astray, or so that if they were injured we could make sure that suitable medical assistance could be provided. The pupils would still be exploring, they would still learn new things (including some we didn't intend) but they would do so in much safer circumstances and could concentrate more about how to read a map rather than worrying about their own safety.

Your pupils want to feel safe to explore; and you need to ensure that they don't waste their time or suffer from information overload. Having too much information is a significant concern when allowing pupils to explore for the first time. Providing guidance through activities such as webquests (see later in this chapter) and providing training for pupils in exploration techniques should allow them to explore information and find out new items whilst preventing the frustrations which come from having so much information that they become unsure of what is relevant and what is not.

CASE STUDY: USE OF ICT IN THE CURRICULUM

A Year 7 History class is studying the First World War. The pupils take ICT as a discrete subject and have been introduced to the software Inspiration (see Software at the end of this chapter) to help them sort out their ideas. The teacher has divided them up into smaller groups of five pupils and they are going to produce some web pages about the life of a soldier in the trenches. The teacher has already used some more traditional sources of information with pupils, such as books and video, but she now wants them to move into an area in which they discover things for themselves. The pupils discuss the topic in detail and the work they have already done. They are then encouraged to think about what they would like to find out more about. They then plan how they will

---

get the information (including both written sources and internet sites they have looked at earlier). The pupils use their plan to help them explore the topic and to make the web pages they are required to produce as part of the activity. The teacher is on hand to help if they go off track.

COMMENTARY ON CASE STUDY

The use of programs and techniques which help children to organise their ideas and think carefully about what they need to do and how to go about it is a preparatory step to a successful exploration. What was good about this case was that the children knew what they were looking for, were encouraged to think about the topic and the requirements placed on them, and were encouraged to plan the exploration rather than just being given a blank sheet and told to go to a site to explore a topic.

Children require support when they are exploring for themselves and as a teacher, you will need to ensure that children have thought through their ideas about what they need to find out and where to explore. This support needs to be made available if pupils are to do more than flounder about in the dark getting lost, or suffer from information overload.

There is a wide range of software which can help children to explore, but it is crucial for you to know the software well enough that you can also guide and support children who are using it.

Activity 8.1 Programs for exploring

1   Write down three programs that would help children to explore.

_____

_____

_____

2   Outline how the programs could be used to help children with their exploration.

- Before they start to explore.

_____

- While they are exploring.

_____

- After they have explored.

_____

WHAT CAPABILITIES WILL WE NEED TO EXPLORE EFFECTIVELY?

The basic skills both staff and pupils will need to master are 'how to think' and 'how to investigate'. If you are not already a master of 'thinking skills', it is important to understand the techniques involved so that you can help pupils to think more effectively. Thinking is something we all do, and the danger of 'training people to think' is that their minds become uniform, and this may not always be desirable. However, an understanding of how to teach thinking skills and critical thinking are important if exploration is to be a viable tool in your classroom.

CASE STUDY: 16+ PUPILS EXPLORING ACCESS

A group of GCE ICT pupils need to learn about Microsoft Access and their teacher has prepared a database to help them to explore the features of Access – in particular the use of modules. The model can be explored through pupils running modules and macros. A password is provided for pupils to enable them to access the model, and the passwords placed on the modules are also provided.

COMMENTARY ON CASE STUDY

Care must be taken in providing this type of model, as it is important that examination regulations are not broken and that pupils do not simply submit it as their own in an adapted form. Pupils could be given the task of finding out what each module does and how it works, and be allowed to explore the model in groups.

Activity 8.2 Planning before an exploration

You want a group of Year 12 pupils to explore the features of Macromedia Dreamweaver and produce some training materials which could be used with future Year 9 pupils.

1   Plan the steps you, as a teacher, would need to undertake before allowing pupils to embark on the activity.

_____

_____

_____

2   Plan what preparation the pupils would need to do before you allowed them to explore the software.

_____

_____

_____

There is no right answer to this activity, but there are certainly wrong answers including 'I would just let the pupils get on with it' or 'Exploring should be about the moment and getting lost is just part of it'. The reality is that when pupils are lost they aren't engaged in the activity or doing anything productive. All they discover is that they are lost and bored with exploring. So:

- Decide on your objectives and what you want pupils to discover.
- Prepare some basic materials for pupils. Give them some starting points and basic details about what you expect from them in terms of product. In this case you may provide example guides produced in previous years or prepared by you. You may give them a range of topics to choose from to investigate.

- Teach or review thinking skills already learnt in other classes, such as classifying and summarising (DfES, 2004b) to help them explore in a meaningful way. Question them about what they are doing, keep them on track.
- Encourage your pupils to use software that will help them organise their ideas (such as Inspiration) and plan their exploration.

Activity 8.3   Explore for yourself

Plan an exploration for yourself in some software that you do not know well, to prepare to teach pupils about it. What would you do to explore the software?

_____
_____
_____

Here are some suggested responses:

- Try the software at home first and use help files.
- Talk to a colleague who has used the software.
- Buy and use a book to improve your skills.
- Prepare some materials to help you to show pupils how to use it.
- Test it on more than one school computer, and with the access rights pupils have. Check that they can download any files and that their view of the software is what you show them; if not, change your materials.

Activity 8.4   Adding exploration to a lesson

Reflect on one lesson you have already taught where you think exploration would have added to the pupils' experience. Assuming that you are to take the lesson again:

1   Plan for the exploration (explore the topic yourself, plan how you will help pupils prepare for their exploration, prepare the guidance you will give to pupils).

_____
_____
_____
_____
_____

2   Plan the support you will need to give pupils.

_____
_____
_____
_____
_____

WHAT DOES TECHNOLOGY BRING TO THE CONCEPT OF 'EXPLORING'?

Almost twenty-five years ago, I played a game with the intriguing title of UKMCR81. The purpose of the game was for you to play the role of the Chancellor of the Exchequer – a modern equivalent is described on a website listed after Further reading at the end of this chapter. You could control government spending and taxation, although very little else. The model used was that of the Treasury and you could use your knowledge of the multiplier and other economic variables to keep the economy on a good path. This particular exercise used a model and provided a simulation of the real world: you could find yourself replaced at a General Election if you didn't do well enough! My teacher allowed us to explore the game for ourselves in our study time in school, but we had already obtained the basic knowledge required to participate effectively from his lessons on macroeconomics. We were not just told to find out about the economics, using the game. What did this give us that could not have been gained from a paper and pen exercise or a practical example?

The following points are not exhaustive but give an indication of why computers are used so widely for exploration:

- People would not like their real-life economic prosperity affected by a group of A-level students.
- There are time-lags in real life between an economic event and the consequences of it becoming apparent.
- Models can help us to understand things that can otherwise be more abstract or even dangerous (you wouldn't want an A-level Physics pupil blowing up a nuclear power station during an experiment).
- Models allow us to keep some variables stable and to see the effect of each item we change – this is not possible in the real world.
- Pupils can work in teams and discuss the scenario and possible solutions.
- Models can simplify a real-life situation to the basic elements required to be understood without the distraction of irrelevant detail.
- The computer can prevent the monotony of continuous calculation and bring in surprise elements that make the model behave more like the real world.
- The model can be explored through the use of different approaches to allow pupils to go into detail about some particular aspect.

CASE STUDY: KS4 PUPILS INVESTIGATE

Pupils in a group have learned about hardware and software types and undertaken a webquest set by their teacher to help them investigate the types in more detail. They are given the task of producing an expert system using Intermodeller (see Software at the end of this chapter). They need to understand the items and present the information in new ways.

COMMENTARY ON CASE STUDY

The pupils in this scenario had already learned the theory but were being asked for a different type of solution. The use of a decision tree should make the ideas easier to grasp for those with a visual disposition, and enable the whole group to go further than merely digesting the facts already taught. The idea is that they think about what they are learning and put it into new formats. The pupils have been shown how to use the software prior to being asked to use it. You should consider creating webquests for your pupils – an example of a webquest can be found at the website listed at the end of this chapter.

Activity 8.5   Five things to model

Consider five things in a GCSE syllabus that you might ask pupils to model and what you would expect pupils to learn from doing this.

_____
_____
_____
_____
_____
_____
_____
_____
_____
_____
_____
_____

Much of the work at GCSE level requires pupils to remember facts and understand the concepts which underly the skills. For example:

- Pupils sometimes find databases and spreadsheets so similar that they mix them up.
- The role of different types of memory within a computer need to be clear.
- Peripheral devices must be categorised as input, output and storage, and the use of different types of each device must be understood.
- Network types need to be identified.

Compiling an expert system may assist them in understanding the distinctions between the items being compared.

Activity 8.6   A simple expert system

Consider how pupils could be supported in creating a simple expert system using a program such as Intermodeller.

Of course, you will also want your pupils to use spreadsheet models and to create them, using packages such as Excel.

Activity 8.7   Charity concert model

A charity concert is to be held at the school you are working in and pupils are to prepare a model showing the profit, loss and breakeven point of the event. How do you prepare your pupils for this activity?

_____
_____

You could specifically plan to develop pupils' independent learning. Pupils need to learn independence in learning as they progress through their secondary school. One way to achieve this is to scaffold the knowledge they need. Activities to prepare pupils for this task should include the following:

- Modelling good practice – showing pupils a model on a similar topic to show them how it can be used to explore.
- Explaining the use of different terms – for example, profit, loss and breakeven.
- Arranging to visit the venue (for example, the school theatre) to allow pupils to find things out in an authentic manner.
- Setting up groups to allow discussion of what was found.
- Reflective plenary sessions.
- Asking pupils to create smaller models that build into the larger one.

This is not a one-lesson activity; scaffolding the knowledge that pupils need will take a series of lessons.

HOW CAN WE DEVELOP OUR PUPILS' ABILITY TO EXPLORE THROUGH TARGETED ACTIVITIES IN SCHOOL?

The DfES has provided some guidance for teachers within the National Strategy on how they believe thinking skills should be incorporated into the classroom. The experience of teachers often echoes the DfES statement that 'pupils do not readily transfer their learning from lesson to lesson and often see little connection between lessons and their life beyond school' (DfES, 2005b: 9). Curriculum managers in schools have been advised to think about using a sequence of lessons within different subjects to help pupils to see how thinking skills can be applied outside the subject in which they are taught (DfES, 2005b). Hence we should work with our colleagues in other subjects to develop these skills more effectively, and we should also aim to use the skills within our own subject.

At first sight, thinking skills and exploration may not appear to be aligned. The DfES states that 'the five thinking skills . . . are: Information processing, Reasoning, Enquiry, Creative thinking [and] Evaluation' (DfES, 2005b: 9). Within ICT lessons, pupils are encouraged to use these thinking skills but the use of exploration allows pupils to use all of these skills within one activity.

CASE STUDY: KEY STAGE 3 PUPILS PLAN A NEW VISIT

A high school organises activities and visits for Year 9 and Year 10 pupils at the end of each year during 'Activities Week'. The teacher who organises the event delegates some of the work to her colleagues who lead particular activities. One year she asked the ICT department to work with the new Year 9 pupils to get some new ideas about what could be done. The purpose of the task as far as the ICT team are concerned is to look at the existing ICT skills of pupils, to note where they have strengths and weaknesses and to help pupils to improve, using a real-life case study.

In their ICT lessons, Year 9 pupils are to go through the planning of a visit. In some cases, where the idea is novel and the interest in the topic is sufficient, the visit may be included on the list of the out-of-school activities, and the work done in class used by the teacher responsible.

COMMENTARY ON CASE STUDY

The activity undertaken by the pupils was authentic; the ideas that pupils produced were considered and some of the pupil work was used in practice (although usually with alteration).

This was an introduction to the concept of exploring, and the exploration was simply part of the activity. It did require a lot of preparatory work with pupils before they embarked fully on the exploration. They needed to be given example activities used in previous years, encouraged to think about a range of possible areas, to isolate their ideas to one topic that they would look at in detail and to find out how they would get more information. The pupils concerned had not received any thinking skills training prior to this and hence the thinking skills that were being taught were integrated into the activity in a non-threatening way.

For pupils who had already embarked on thinking skills courses, the skills would simply be reinforced by this type of activity. This is just a straightforward technique that could be used in almost any classroom for any subject.

Activity 8.8 Five topics for exploration

1   Write down five topics where exploration could make the subject of ICT more interesting.
2   Write down what steps you would need to do as a teacher to prepare pupils to explore each of the topics you have outlined.
3   Write down any barriers to using exploration with your pupils.
4   Write down how those barriers can be overcome.

Think carefully about the following argument: 'Children should be taught to explore before they begin an activity rather than within an activity.'

This is the view of de Bono (1996) and other writers who believe that you should teach people to think before you expect them to apply thinking skills. In either case, you should not think of pupils as empty vessels concerning the skill of exploration – they have been exploring all their lives! You need to ensure that the opportunities you provide for exploration develop further the skills that pupils have already, and allow them to learn new techniques of thinking.

Thinking skills are becoming an increasing feature of the secondary school classroom and you should investigate them and use them in your teaching. It is too easy to focus on what we want pupils to learn and forget that we want them to also learn to be more independent. Simply passing on our knowledge is not sufficent; we need to make sure our pupils can learn things for themselves. We wouldn't expect a four-year-old to walk to school by themselves, but an eleven-year-old might reasonably be expected to get to school independently. This greater independence is the result of scaffolded knowledge (of traffic, timetables, etc.) and greater experience. Similarly, we need to scaffold the techniques of thinking that will help pupils to get more out of their learning.

But do not confuse independent learning with working individually. As Vygotsky states,

> learning awakens a variety of internal developmental processes that are able to operate only when the child is interacting with people in his environment and in cooperation with his peers. Once these processes are internalized, they become part of the child's independent developmental achievement.
>
> (1978: 90)

Working within a group setting may help a child to learn and understand more due to the communication between group members. But this will happen only if you work with pupils to ensure that all pupils in the group participate and that all learn.

It is crucial that you prepare thoroughly for the exploration activities you will do in your classroom. If you do prepare the activity thoroughly, then it is likely that you will be pleased with the results of the lesson.

SUMMARY

ICT has an important contribution to make to the development of thinking skills, and the right ICT tools can help students to apply their thinking skills across the curriculum to explore new ideas effectively. This will not happen automatically, however, and it is therefore important to make this aspect of learning ICT explicit in your teaching.

FURTHER READING

AEL/Inspiration (2003) *Graphic Organizers: A Review of Scientifically Based Research*, Charleston, WV: AEL and Portland, OR: Inspiration. Available at http://www.inspiration.com/download/pdf/SBR_summary.pdf

De Bono, E. (1996) *Teach Yourself to Think*, London: Penguin.

Daniels, H. (2001) *Vygotsky and Pedagogy*, London: Routledge.

DfES (2003) *Key Stage 3 Strategy, Foundation Subjects Strand: Key Messages about Teaching Thinking*, London: DfES.

DfES (2004) *Pedagogy and Practice: Teaching and Learning in Secondary Schools: Unit 17: Developing Effective Learning*, London: DfES.

DfES (2005) *Leading in Learning: Exemplification in ICT*, London: DfES.

Lavonen, J. *et al.* (2003) 'Concretising the programming task: a case study in a secondary school', *Computers and Education* 40, 115–135.

WEBSITES

UK economy simulation: www.economicsnetwork.ac.uk/handbook/games/41.htm
Webquests: www.webquestuk.org.uk/ (provides a link to the original webquest.org site).

SOFTWARE

Inspiration: www.inspiration.com
Intermodeller: www.parlog.com.

Part 3　Your development as a teacher of ICT

This section of the book explores the broad question of how do you become a better teacher of ICT. Chapter 9 focuses on subject knowledge. It explains the importance of updating your subject knowledge and the difference between knowledge of application and knowledge for teaching.

The chapter is making two very important points. First, your existing knowledge of ICT is unlikely to cover everything that you need to be a confident teacher of ICT. This is because of changes in ICT as a subject; changes in hardware and software provision; and the gap between what your degree has covered and what you are expected to teach. Second, subject knowledge is a much broader term than you might have thought. It covers what you know about ICT and how computer applications are used but it also includes your understanding of the school curriculum, for example, how ICT is organised at KS3 and the options within the increasingly diverse qualifications framework. Subject knowledge further covers what you know about the teaching of specific topics, which aspects of these topics pupils find difficult and how best to address the misconceptions which they hold.

If you find the task of gaining the required level of subject knowledge in its widest sense to be quite daunting, try to take a positive approach and treat all your experience as an opportunity to learn. You come to teaching with a wide range of skills and experiences and your aim is to become an intelligent practitioner, open about your areas to develop, alert to pupils' learning and aware of what they are required to learn. You are not required to be a computing virtuoso, and these final two chapters present you with strategies for developing the subject knowledge you require. If there is a single theme, it is 'try it out and reflect on what happened'. There is a place for ploughing through manuals and self-help guides in order to gain mastery of specific techniques, but subject knowledge for teaching often involves trying things out in real-life settings. For example, try developing resources with colleagues for topics in which your subject knowledge is weak; teach small groups so that you can monitor the difficulties they experience and the impact of your interventions; visit a workplace where you can see up-to-date ICT applications and consider the implications for the courses you teach.

Chapter 10 continues the theme of developing your teaching by looking at planning teaching and assessment as other areas for development, both during your training and as an NQT. It counsels against simply 'learning by practice'; you will surely get better the more you teach, but this alone is not enough. The chapter asks you to commit yourself to systematic professional development by following a learning cycle in which you identify a problem to address, look at potential solutions, select a solution that works for you; and evaluate the solution you have implemented. As in Chapter 4, it asks you to follow such cycles as a matter of routine. In your first year of teaching there appears an impressive array of support available for you to develop as a teacher, but choosing the right school is a key consideration here. A detailed case study shows how the support of a head of department, an induction tutor, local authority provision, visits out of school and peer observation in school all helped one teacher to master the basic skills essential for her development and to develop her teaching repertoire in an impressive manner. However none of this support would have been of any use without this teacher's ability to identify an area to develop and her commitment to change.

It is easy to see that a theme of this section of the book is change; you are developing your practice at the same time as the nature of your subject is changing. Anyone teaching ICT in recent years has seen new vocational qualifications come and go. ICT as a subject has become firmly established. Whole-class teaching is commonplace in schools where once pupils were more or less left alone to work (or play) at machines; online testing has been introduced; web page design has moved from being an exotic extra to a taken-for-granted activity; internet access is the norm, with all that implies for communication and access to material; and there have been large-scale innovations, such as the Key Stage 3 Strategy and 'Success for All' at post-16, which have tried to make lasting changes in the teaching of ICT. It is safe to predict that as you enter teaching you will see further changes and, while we cannot know with any certainty the nature of these changes, there are some indications of trends. These provide the basis for six predictions offered below about the future of ICT teaching in school. However, as you start to develop your career as an ICT teacher, think about your own agenda for change and where you want to see our subject go in the future.

Prediction 1: You will be called on to develop the use of ICT across the curriculum

There is no doubt that the teaching of ICT has much improved in schools and no doubt that teaching ICT as a separate subject is core to extending pupils' ICT capability. However, there has not been such consistent advance in using ICT across the curriculum, and this can be expected to be a continuing concern if the investment in ICT is going to be seen as worthwhile. As a new ICT teacher, expect to be called on to contribute to whole-school policies on using ICT, including the search for solutions to provide access to technology which do not require block bookings of ICT suites. You can prepare for this future role by working with colleagues from different subjects during your training and into your first year in school. To carry out this role successfully you will need to be a good listener, and work on small sustainable incremental projects. Many teachers feel that by merely using the interactive whiteboard, they are achieving a goal of embedding ICT into the curriculum. They will need subtle persuasion and evidence of the potential for learning when pupils use ICT, both independently and collaboratively. Your role is to support the subject specialist's agenda and this will require patience if, as will certainly happen, you see there are some tools which are not being used. When you find yourself getting frustrated with the pace of change, reflect on your own response to cross-curricular initiatives such as literacy and citizenship!

Prediction 2: You will be called on to overhaul the National Strategy

The units within the KS3 strategy were designed as exemplars of teaching the subject, not a course book to be followed. The units were produced some time ago and are not tailored to particular circumstances, yet many schools are rigidly following the units as they first appeared. If this is still happening in your school you have an urgent job of renewal and innovation on your hands! Part 2 of this book provides a valuable alternative perspective.

Prediction 3: You will be expected to provide greater coherence between the KS3 curriculum and the qualifications framework for 14–19

Whatever its shortcomings, the National Strategy for ICT offers a balanced curriculum with elements of creativity, prediction, exploration and communication. In contrast, many of the ICT qualifications on offer are excessively focused on business applications of ICT, particularly databases, spreadsheets and data processing in general. They tend to pay little attention to multimedia, gaming and communications technology. The picture is changing – expect it to change a lot more.

Prediction 4: You will be asked to contribute to the creativity agenda in school

Creativity is about taking steps to give pupils opportunities to use their imagination to express themselves, and make original and valued choices in their lives (Loveless, 2002). There are repeated concerns that the curriculum has become too prescriptive and has stifled the creativity of both teachers and learners. No government is going to sanction a move towards a 'free for all' but there is going to be pressure on schools to give pupils greater choice. This is not simply because choice is a 'nice' thing to offer pupils, but because creativity, and the development of a large creative industry sector, lies at the core of future economic prosperity. As seen in Chapter 5, ICT can make a distinctive contribution to creativity in school by supporting imaginative expression, for example in making original and eye-catching multimedia presentations and short films that give voice to pupils' interests and in developing unique solutions to problems of control and monitoring.

Prediction 5: You will be asked to contribute to the personalised learning agenda

The present government in England is proposing a personalised learning agenda to address diversity: each child comes to school with a unique mix of knowledge and skill, particular aptitudes and aspirations and preferences for particular modes of teaching and learning (DfES, 2005b). ICT is important here as many pupils find it difficult to access a traditional academic curriculum in which normal practice is to work from paper texts and train for timed pen-and-paper testing in school halls. Personalised learning with ICT should not be seen as classes of pupils working in a computer room, wearing headphones and being programmed individually with the prescribed curriculum that they are required to reproduce at examination time. However, ICT does have a key role to play in promoting personalised learning: by providing opportunities for vocational as well as academic routes; by making teaching and learning with images and multimedia resources routine; and by providing pupils with resources which they can access anywhere and at anytime.

Prediction 6: You will be asked to contribute to mobile (m-) learning initiatives

M-learning is entering the vocabulary to focus attention on mobile technologies (such as mobile phones and hand-held computers) in teaching and learning (Ultralab, 2005). Mobile technologies impact on what we teach and how we teach it. The most familiar technology for most young people is the mobile phone which at the time of writing is being reinvented as a music player, a provider of access to the internet, a storage device for programs and files and a 'video calling' communications device. The most common database which pupils use is the 'address book' on the mobile phone, which holds their friends' numbers, or the list of tracks on their iPods. We are challenged to use these and other examples from pupils' day-to-day experience to illustrate our teaching of IT concepts, while recognising that not all pupils have access to this technology. We are further challenged to use mobile technology for teaching and learning access to our own online resources, podcasts and communications. The point of m-learning is that it it exploits the tools that young people use routinely and, though crucially not in all cases, overcomes issues of access.

ICT has an almost unique connection with many pupils' needs and interests. This can be exploited for both our own and our pupils' benefit. We can best do this by giving pupils insight into what they do, and pushing their creative use of the new technology; this is not imitating what pupils do outside of school but extending it. To do this successfully means building on core skills developed within your training; to know when to direct pupils and when to give them choices; to value whole-class teaching as well as small group and collaborative working; to know how to prepare pupils to be successful in gaining existing qualifications but to identify opportunities for offering more relevant qualifications. To keep up with changes, let alone lead change in school, is going to be a tremendous challenge. If this can seem an overwhelming prospect, the contrast is to find yourself teaching the same topics in the same way in five or even ten years time – and who would opt for that?

Chapter 9  Developing your ICT capability and knowledge for teaching

IAN HUGHES AND STEVE KENNEWELL

INTRODUCTION

In this chapter we will look at:

- why you need to update knowledge and skills;
- the difference between knowledge for application and knowledge for teaching;
- the changing nature of ICT as a subject;
- different strategies to develop your subject knowledge.

By the end of this chapter you should be able to:

- identify aspects of ICT for which you need to develop your knowledge and skills;
- gain support for broadening and deepening your subject knowledge for teaching;
- understand the need to continue the process throughout your career.

THE NEED TO UPDATE KNOWLEDGE AND SKILLS

Every trainee taking a course of initial teacher education in ICT as a specialism will have some knowledge of ICT, but this will have developed through different sets of experiences. On your course you may meet graduates in Computer Science; graduates of Business Studies, Engineering or even Media Studies courses with a high ICT content; people with joint degrees in IT and English or Sports Studies; people with degrees in unrelated subjects who have converted to Computer Science at masters level; and people who have received equivalent training during employment. Many of your fellow trainees will have learnt much of their ICT through self-study and experimentation, and may not have experienced formal 'textbook' approaches to theoretical topics.

This means that everyone needs to develop their subject knowledge in order to be confident in teaching the full range of courses at school level. Developing and updating subject knowledge will be familiar to you if you have recently completed courses of study in ICT or have been keeping up with new ideas in your employment, but learning to teach involves more than merely filling gaps in your knowledge. There is a fundamental difference now in how you should approach your study of new topics or revision of familiar ones – you are learning for the purposes of teaching ICT, rather than applying ICT to information-handling problems.

You might start by reflecting on your experiences prior to the start of your training course. Consider the case of Anji who has been working as an analyst programmer, with a strong feeling of control over computer systems and an ability to build software environments to requirements specified by users. She wants to share that feeling with youngsters; she knows they have used sophisticated software written by others all their lives (particularly games and Office software) and she would like to teach them the formal techniques they need to produce software themselves.

As she observes lessons in a school, she realises that this sort of work does not seem to have a place in ICT courses, even at A level where Computing has been discontinued because it is seen as too narrow in scope. She notices that the youngsters seem to pick up techniques by trial and error, and that once a pupil has discovered something, it quickly spreads around the class. Carefully prepared handouts, on the other hand, may be ignored and quickly discarded. Most classes have pupils who have considerable expertise in certain aspects of ICT. She notices that other pupils (and even the teacher!) often turn to these 'experts' for advice.

Her tutors explain the idea of ICT capability, and the need for experience and competence with a range of types of ICT activity. She understands the key concepts which support the application of ICT tools to the sort of tasks that the general ICT user will meet, such as presentation, audience, search, 'what if', accuracy, and safety. She realises that pupils in school have very limited experience of financial and administrative systems, and that even to produce simple databases and spreadsheets can be a challenge if they have no practical experience of profit and loss, customers and suppliers, invoices and payments.

She finds that she is expected to relate her ICT teaching to the rest of the curriculum, yet the sort of work pupils might use ICT for in History or Modern Languages seems quite trivial. The GCSE ICT course seems to involve a lot of writing of text, but relatively little attention to recent developments in technology. She finds that many post-16 courses have an emphasis on business and management issues rather than requiring a detailed knowledge of computer and communication systems.

Anji discovers that her subject knowledge has developed in a particular sphere, and her particular knowledge and skills do not cover all that is required for the ICT National Curriculum. Her experience is of highly structured ICT processes and training, which is very different to the way pupils see ICT and their approach to learning, which is often 'playing around' and through asking how to do things when they need to do them.

Anji was able to re-focus her perceptions and ideas as she moved through her training, taking account of the experience and abilities of the pupils concerning aspects such as audience and purpose, which she previously took for granted. With experience, she was able to adjust how to approach her own learning with that required to present the ideas to her pupils in a way that enabled them to understand concepts and retain facts and skills. Furthermore, Anji was able to utilise her own experience and expertise to enrich her teaching of the subject, even within the restrictions of the examination syllabuses and KS3 strategy which impose many constraints on the approaches to teaching and learning.

THE NATURE OF ICT AS A SUBJECT

Unlike most subjects, the continual development of the technology leads to constant change in content. On one hand this means that you cannot know everything, and this is not expected. What becomes increasingly important is not so much what you know about a topic, but your willingness to learn new skills, to be open to advice and not to hide your ignorance of relevant knowledge. Regular reading of educational, professional and hobby literature in ICT will be important throughout your teaching career, as well as attending local, regional and national conferences (such as those run by Naace, the ICT subject association); exhibitions such as British Education and Training Technology (BETT) and examination board seminars.

On the other hand, you cannot rely on picking it all up as you go along; there is a substantial body of knowledge and skills that you do need, which often provides the basis for audits and target setting throughout your training (see, for example, Kennewell et al, 2003: Appendix). These audits will lead you to consider your strengths and the aspects which need development in the two areas dealt with below.

Your understanding of the nature and scope of courses and the interpretation of key concepts and processes embedded within them

You will need a thorough understanding of the nature and scope of the ICT National Curriculum attainment target and the programmes of study. Kennewell *et al.*, (2003) discuss these matters further in general terms, and details of the NC can be found in government materials to be found on websites such as the KS3 National Strategy, National Curriculum in Action and QCA (see details of websites at the end of the chapter.) The previous sections on creativity etc. within this book will help you further appreciate underlying principles associated with ICT.

You will need to be familiar with the 'theory' of ICT, up to a level determined by the age range of your course and your own aspirations for a teaching post. You will need to gain a good understanding of aspects of both general and vocational courses. However extensive your own knowledge is, you still need to know how to interpret the syllabus in the way expected by the examinations board. It is a good idea to try an examination paper for which you have access to the mark scheme. When you review your answers in relation to the mark scheme, consider what the examiners were focusing on. Compare this with your expectations of the answer and the key points; perhaps your answers have greater depth. Confusion over examination questions often comes from a greater knowledge than that expected of the candidates. The greater the variety of question papers and published mark schemes you attempt, the greater the feeling for the depth of knowledge required you will achieve. This will help you advise pupils on the retention of facts that need to be recalled in examinations and on techniques for answering questions. You will also need to gain an understanding of progression in pupil learning across Years 7–13: the same ideas may occur in the National Curriculum, GCSE and A-level courses, but the depth of understanding and the complexity of application will increase. See Chapter 4 and Kennewell *et al.* (2003) for further discussion of progression.

Practical skills and coursework experience

You need to understand the structure of the projects which pupils carry out at all levels of the curriculum, particularly the design process. Often coursework has two aspects associated with it; the practical skills aspect and the systems analysis development of a holistic solution to a problem where the practical skills aspect is secondary. Examination boards and publishers such as Payne-Gallway (see Websites at the end of this chapter) produce guides and exemplar materials for particular schemes which could form the basis of your own resources. Consider two key questions – 'What is the examiner expecting?' and 'How can you enable the pupils to comprehend this and produce the required materials?' Working through exemplar materials will enable you to get an idea about the first question, but the second is far more difficult as pupils come with little experience and a range of possible misconceptions about the GCSE course. Attempt a project for yourself, using the software which will be available in school in order to get a feel for the requirements. This will also help you to subdivide a seemingly huge task for pupils into manageable tasks. These will vary according to the focus of qualification and the abilities and interests of the pupils to be taught. It will also help you to work out a schedule for completion of various aspects of the coursework.

You should also seek to understand the basic network configuration and components found in a typical school, and to find out how school technicians and network managers enable teachers and pupils to use the network effectively in teaching and learning. Make sure that you have mastered the hardware and software commonly currently used in teaching, such as interactive whiteboards and associated software.

You will need a detailed knowledge of the various packages that will be used and taught in the classroom, covering the concepts underlying them, the contexts in which they are used, the processes they are designed to carry out and the techniques used to achieve these processes. You will need to develop knowledge of how such skills and concepts are exemplified in the classroom to various levels of pupil age, ability and interest. You will need to think carefully about those techniques which you carry out without conscious thought (routines) and consider the need to demonstrate and explain them to pupils (see Kennewell *et al.,* (2003) for further discussion of processes, techniques and routines). The best way to represent ideas will vary according to the pupils' abilities and ages. You may be expected to demonstrate methods which are different from those which you would use; they may not be the most efficient methods but there is usually a reason for this. For example, in many Microsoft packages, you should teach pupils to use File and then Print rather than the print button, as pupils will tend to double-click the button or click many times when nothing seems to happen, with the result that many copies of the same thing are produced, and possibly by the wrong printer.

Up-to-date knowledge is essential because many pupils are likely to know about the latest developments in technology or have trawled the internet to find an obscure driver or utility program. Whilst you cannot be expected to have detailed knowledge of this, you should at least be able to converse knowledgeably about the principles and be prepared take the role of a learner or co-learner in matters where your knowledge is weak. Most pupils are very skilled in the use of mobile phone and messaging technology; although this field is poorly represented in formal curricula, it represents a source of knowledge that it will be valuable to draw on in order to raise pupils' critical awareness. Developing an understanding of new technologies will maintain your interest in the subject, as well as improving your credibility with pupils. What you know about your pupils' knowledge is also important (Webb, 2002, and see Chapter 1 of this book).

You may need to develop new skills for particular courses, and additionally you should be aware of which skills are specifically required to fulfil the course that is to be taught. The examination boards will monitor developments in technology and will incorporate aspects in future examination papers. For example, at the time of writing the 'chip and pin' method of electronic funds transfer is becoming universal so is soon likely to be part of examination papers.

Activity 9.1 New developments and examination syllabuses

Identify a new technology or recent controversial issue that you think will soon be required as part of examination syllabuses, and investigate sources of training and support.

Discuss whether examiners should try to anticipate important new developments and include them in the syllabus which may be formulated years in advance of when the relevant examination will be taken.

STRATEGIES TO DEVELOP YOUR SUBJECT KNOWLEDGE

In order to develop your knowledge, you may use a variety of approaches in college sessions, in school and through independent study. For example, in college, you could take advantage of opportunities for peer group tutoring, perhaps producing help sheets for your colleagues or identifying strengths in a group and 'trading' skills and knowledge (see Case study 1 below, for example). In school, you might carry out tasks aimed at various ages and levels, observe and talk to pupils in order to gain awareness of their knowledge, create worksheets on other resources for different pupil abilities (see Case study 2 later in this chapter), and seek advice from your mentor concerning the emphasis needed for different aspects of schemes of work. You can also consult textbooks and revision guides to obtain insight into what is expected at particular levels and look at examination board exemplar questions and mark schemes. There are websites which provide useful guides and resources (see details at the end of this chapter) and you may also be able to make contact with local businesses or other organisations to help update and broaden your knowledge (see Case studies 3 and 4).

CASE STUDY: TRAINEE TEACHER 1

Bethan is a Business Studies graduate who has worked for two years within a team developing databases for a large company. She is gaining deeper knowledge of A-level Computing theory topics through developing resources as part of a team. Bethan has strengths in social aspects and the design and interrrogation of databases, but very little experience in the hardware, operating system or programming elements of the syllabus.

Bethan's tutor has split the ICT PGCE into groups, each containing trainees with different strengths and weaknesses in their knowledge. They were required to develop teaching and learning resources for topics within an identified A-level ICT syllabus. The topic allocated to Bethan's team is a coursework element, consisting of developing a database with a Visual Basic user interface front end. There are a number of aspects that have to be considered:

- The problem scenario, the solution to the problem and a breakdown of its requirements.
- The pupils' experiences in terms of systems analysis, databases, Visual Basic and general experiences of user interfaces and in relation to the scenario.
- The information that the pupils will need in order to solve the problem.
- The learning that will enable them to solve other problems of this type. With all this in mind, the task of solving the problem is split between the team, based on their perceived strengths, so that Bethan picks up the database design aspects. Looking at the exemplar materials from the examination board and advice from her tutor, it becomes obvious that the level at which Bethan is basing her solution is too high for the content of the syllabus and the requirements of the pupils. This is also the case for the other members of the group in their aspects of the topic.

The group decides to list in detail the requirements indicated by the syllabus and the materials. They gain a clearer view of what is expected and simplify the solution to the problem whilst still meeting the requirements of the scheme. One of the tutors has experience in marking coursework and is able to give a general guide to the grade the solution would attain. After some amendments, the second aspect of the resource development has to be considered: pupils' knowledge. The group is able to subdivide the requirements into learning objectives for each aspect, assuming basic GCSE knowledge and a progression from the assumed GCSE knowledge to the requirement to solve the problem.

Each member of the group undertakes to develop a learning resource in the area in which they feel weakest so that they would learn as they developed the resource. Bethan is able to act as mentor to her colleague who is developing a scenario description for the problem and to another who is writing guidelines on database design. She is able to draw on expertise from the other members of the team concerning her own resource development which is a guide to Visual Basic.

The resources were mainly 'how to' guides and writing frames. The group considered how these would be presented to the pupils. They discuss each aspect of the solution and the relevant resources in turn, with consideration of a variety of teaching strategies. They formulate appropriate ways of teaching each aspect, and the team members who developed each resource draw up lesson plans. The resulting lesson plans and resources are shown to a tutor for comment, and tested on a peer group. They decide to present one or two standard scenarios and solutions and ask the pupils to write a short synopsis of their problem after initial investigative work. These will then be discussed individually with each pupil.

Finally, they collate the resources for each topic of the module and write an initial guide to the module resources. These form part of the resource for the whole syllabus that each trainee is able to take and use.

COMMENTARY ON CASE STUDY 1

Initially, Bethan's responsibility reflected her strengths, and this helped to highlight her difficulty in determining the depth of the ideas to be covered. Her experience and knowledge was at a higher level that that required by the pupils, and the language that she was using exceeded the level that the pupils would understand. Producing the list of requirements helped the group to focus on what exactly each pupil needed to understand; this was a particularly useful strategy for the trainees in enabling them to identify learning requirements. In the second phase, Bethan was placed in the position of a learner and she was able, to a certain extent, to go through a similar process to that of the pupil and better able to empathise with her target audience. As each member of the group was also responsible for evaluating and providing feedback on the materials to each other member of the group, Bethan was also able to give a 'limited experience' viewpoint on the resources which was invaluable to all in the group. In the third phase, the tutor was on hand to help with interpretation and advise on difficulties often found in the classroom, as part of the initial discussion into teaching strategies and planning. The final resource was not only valuable to the trainees in supporting the teaching of a complete A-level syllabus but also contained a wide variety of teaching strategies which could be transferred to other situations that the trainees might encounter.

Activity 9.2 Supporting an A-level ICT syllabus

Download an A-level ICT syllabus from one of the examination boards (AQA, OCR, Edexcel, WJEC). Choose a particular section and produce your own detailed list of knowledge and skill requirements, using textbooks, websites, and tutor and mentor advice to help. For one or more aspects of the list, produce some material, for example an electronic worksheet, which helps pupils learn and enables you to check their understanding. Ask a colleague with greater knowledge of this field to comment on its accuracy and completeness, and revise if necessary.

CASE STUDY: TRAINEE TEACHER 2

Chris is a Computer Science graduate who has a good knowledge of programming but little experience of communication and multimedia work. During his second teaching practice session, the ICT department to which he was attached decides to introduce video editing to some of the ICT examination classes for a multimedia unit. To facilitate this, the department sets up a training session where an advisory teacher is asked to demonstrate the use of the package; this is recorded on video to enable the teachers to review it later. In consultation with the Head of Department, Chris lists the skills/knowledge requirements for the unit and uses the video clips from the training session to develop online teaching media for the pupils. He shows these to the ICT staff who comment on the appropriateness of the resources and discuss possible teaching strategies. Based on this advice, Chris is able to produce lesson plans for the unit. These are checked by the Head of Department before the unit is taught.

COMMENTARY ON CASE STUDY 2

The ideas and processes from the training session were reinforced by the work in the collaborative development of the pupil resources and supporting materials. The work done in conjunction with experienced teachers enabled the trainee both to get to grips with this new package, and to gain knowledge of how it can be presented to a class.

The lesson was very successful, but despite the experience of the mentor, a number of unforeseen events occurred when using the video resources to introduce the new package. The time to download the movie was longer than expected and there was an initial problem with the pupils not having sufficient access to parts of the software. This highlights an important issue; it is essential that anything new is tried out and tested for real. Although it may work in one situation, you need to consider what happens when you log on as a pupil on particular equipment.

The overall outcome was that the trainee gained valuable experience and the school gained a valuable set of resources.

Activity 9.3 Introductory movie demonstration

Decide on a package that you know well and create an *introductory* movie demonstration. Possible software is suggested in Further Reading at the end of Chapter 5. Decide on appropriate assessment criteria for your introductory session. Try the resource on another trainee who has limited or no knowledge of the package. Monitor and assess the results of your colleague using the resource. Evaluate the resource and the assessment criteria.

CASE STUDY: TRAINEE TEACHER 3

Donna is developing her knowledge of assessment procedures for the National Curriculum during college sessions and teaching practice. Many of the trainees on the course have expressed concern over allocating levels to pupils' work, and the tutor asked an ICT coordinator to come in with some samples of work for the trainees to look at and carry out a levelling exercise. Donna found this useful, but she was concerned that she could not judge the level of other work that she would meet in school. To help with this, Donna went through the teaching resources that she had produced and tried to identify aspects of each item that would relate to a particular level. She soon realised that this was more difficult that it first seemed, as there were a number of ambiguities. Donna selected a range of samples and took them to her tutor for clarification. The tutor's advice gave Donna more confidence, but it also raised a number of questions, such as:

- If a pupil has had help to produce a piece of work, how does this affect the level?
- How can a pupil move from one level to the next?
- If a pupil is strong in one element and weak in another, how would a level be given to the pupil?

To answer these and other questions, Donna looked on websites such as the QCA for advice, and the tutor contacted the local advisory service for schools in the area. The whole group of ICT trainees visited the Teachers' Centre and spoke to one of the advisory teachers. Donna looked at some pupils' portfolios that had been assessed as showing evidence for particular levels, so that she could use them as exemplar materials. Donna's mentor was further able to help her in 'target setting' for pupils. This exercise was seen as important from the school point of view, which mirrored that of the county and inspectorate. She was able to shadow the mentor when he interviewed pupils in his class, highlighting the level that they had attained and the criteria for this assessment. Donna noted that pupils were active participants in the interview, and were able to evaluate their work. With prompts from the mentor, each pupil was able to say what they needed to improve and progress. This was noted by the pupil in an evaluation sheet and also recorded by the mentor. Donna found that this gave insight into pupils' learning, which gave her more confidence in her assessment planning. She was able to feed back this to the rest of the group.

COMMENTARY ON CASE STUDY 3

Interpretation of the National Curriculum documents takes practice and experience, and even then the interpretation is often debatable. This is a similar situation to marking coursework for external examinations; the help and support the pupil has received could mean the difference between one grade and level and another, which is why the examination boards and National Curriculum levelling rely heavily on the experience and integrity of the teacher. The simplest way is to estimate the level that the pupil would have achieved if they had carried out the work autonomously. The teacher's experience is crucial here again, as the help could be just a small matter of pointing out a menu item that the pupil had forgotten, so that the pupil succeeded with the small prompt and one could argue that the pupil could attain that particular level. Much of the decision making comes from knowledge of the pupil, which has been formed over a period of time. Levelling can be carried out as a mechanical exercise, but it lacks the accuracy of a comprehensive assessment. The main feature of the assessment that Donna witnessed was the interaction with the pupil. If the pupil has ownership of the assessment process, and is able fully to comprehend the requirements and reasoning behind the assessment, then they are more able to achieve, be motivated and become more autonomous in their learning process. Donna realised that if a pupil goes through an interactive process where they are fully aware of the requirements and can even negotiate an assessment path, then they are more able to become a participant in a process of learning rather than merely the subject of an assessment.

Activity 9.4 Clarifying the National Curriculum

Consider each aspect of the current National Curriculum and suggest how you would amend it to clarify aspects that you believe are unclear.

_____
_____
_____
_____
_____

CASE STUDY: TRAINEE TEACHER 4

Edward is a mature trainee who obtained a degree in Classics in 1984. He worked in programming and systems analysis in the financial services sector and has an excellent knowledge of large administrative systems. He needs to develop his knowledge of real-world applications of control technology. He contacts a water-bottling plant who agree to allow him to view the plant with reference to the ICT side. He takes photographs and materials, and he develops resources from the photographs and literature provided.

The resources tell the story of the bottling plant over time; the statistics and marketing; what is produced and how the assembly line is controlled. These are shown in the form of a presentation by using photo-manipulation software and adding his voice to explain the key points. He also creates diagrams showing the workings of the control systems including the controlling variables that provide the stimulus for computer-aided feedback and control. Edward then goes on to create a simulation, using Flash, to demonstrate the various aspects and what happens when one of the variables changes and how it affects the feedback loop and the corresponding mechanical controls. He combines the video clip created by the photo-presentation software and the Flash animation into a multimedia presentation. He sets up an online test based on a different scenario to establish whether the learnt knowledge is transferable. This gives him some initial feedback as to the success of his material. Edward is able to convert this multi-media presentation into a fully online resource in the form of web pages with the test being carried out online and the results being fed directly into a database.

COMMENTARY ON CASE STUDY 4

Edward had done some initial research using a GCSE textbook and the internet so he had some idea of the level and content required. This helped him focus when he visited the bottling factory, collected the photographic evidence and made notes relating to each photograph for each of the main points:

- What the production line does.
- What variables need to be monitored.
- How they capture the data.
- What processing/decisions are carried out automatically.
- How feedback is communicated.
- What/how information is displayed.

This took the learner through a progression of ideas, finally bringing the whole thing together at the end. In breaking the learning requirements down to their detailed components and using actual examination questions and model answers from the examination board website, Edward was able to get a comprehensive understanding of the control element of the syllabus. This was confirmed when he was able to apply this knowledge and understanding to the new scenario.

The initial piloting and feedback from the assessments provided Edward with information about the pupils' learning and about his approach to teaching. He created a completely stand-alone resource that allowed him to identify areas that needed to be backed up with further teaching. He was also able to amend or rewrite aspects that proved to be less than successful, and re-evaluate some of his teaching strategies.

Activity 9.5 Local company's use of ICT

Contact a local company and ask whether it is possible to arrange a visit and/or collect information related to the use of ICT for a particular purpose in the company. Use this information to develop a resource appropriate for a particular examination course.

SUMMARY

You will have embarked on a course of teacher training with a unique set of experiences on which to base the development of your teaching. There is a need for you to develop an understanding of curriculum knowledge and ways of representing it which is shared with other teachers and which meets certain standards. Your understanding must be sufficiently rich and flexible to allow for adaptation in response to changes in technology, changes in curriculum specifications and changes in pupil experience and ability.

FURTHER READING

Kennewell, S., Parkinson, J. and Tanner, H. (eds) (2003) *Learning to Teach ICT in the Secondary School*, London: RoutledgeFalmer.

Webb, M. (2002) 'Pedagogical reasoning: issues and solutions for the teaching and learning of ICT in secondary schools, *Education and Information Technologies* 7(3): 237–255.

WEBSITES

Interactive learning for ICT GCSE: www.ictgcse.com/.
Key Stage 3 National Strategy: www.standards.dfes.gov.uk/keystage3/subjects.ict
Naace: www.naace.gov.uk
National Curriculum in Action: www.ncaction.org.uk
Payne-Gallway: www.payne-gallway.co.uk/
Qualifications and Curriculum Authority: www.qca.org.uk

Chapter 10 Developing your teaching of ICT

MICHAEL HAMMOND AND JUDE SLAMA

INTRODUCTION

This chapter looks at developing your teaching, adopting a learning cycle approach and finding support as an NQT.

By the end of this chapter you should be able to:

- identify areas to develop;
- outline strategies for developing your teaching;
- consider a proactive approach to Continuing Professional Development within your first year of teaching.

DEVELOPING YOUR TEACHING

How do you get better at teaching? It often seems you get better by practice but it is not as simple as that. With practice you may get more fluent, and pupils will get more used to you and your teaching style, but if you are really going to have a greater impact on pupils' learning you will need to take a close look at your strengths and areas for development. Knowing your strengths will give you a greater sense of confidence and provide structure to the improvement of your teaching. Knowing your areas to develop, and acting on them, will enable you to become a rounded teacher.

How do you recognise an area to develop? They may be all too painful to you through negative feedback from pupils. However you might not be the best judge of your teaching. As teachers we are often slow to recognise strengths and too eager to take responsibility for our shortcomings. Perhaps we misinterpret those shortcomings. For example, many trainee teachers put the difficulties they experience in classroom management down to inexperience and not being forceful enough in the classroom. In part they are right to do so. It is clearly important to establish routines, say for entry and exit to the classroom, to give direction in a confident and assertive manner, and to regularly scan pupils working at machines and intervene to keep them on task. However it is equally important to look at the accessibility of the curriculum and its appeal or lack of appeal for young learners. For example, many youngsters are attracted to ICT as it offers more scope for independent work and appeals to their interest in interactive media. There are considerable opportunities for engaging pupils in ICT lessons which might be missed if you become locked into a narrow focus on classroom management. Other teachers can give you insight into what is going on in your classroom and help you reach a more detached view about addressing the difficulties you are encountering.

There will be several people with a direct responsibility for tutoring or mentoring during your training – for example, an induction tutor, mentor and Higher Education tutors. Ask them to help you to identify areas to develop, to explain the evidence on which they are basing their judgements and to model ways of developing your teaching. Other teachers in your school can offer important input even if they have no formal role in your training. Find colleagues you trust and ask them to observe your lesson or some of your lesson, let them know you would like open and honest feedback on what you are you doing well and where you can develop further. Whatever training programme you are following there will be opportunities for organising peer review from other trainee teachers. These colleagues may lack experience but will often be more understanding and empathetic about your difficulties. If you feel confident enough, talk to the pupils too. They probably will not want to comment on whether you are a 'good teacher' or not, but ask them about the activities in your lesson rather than your performance. For example, ask them if they enjoy whole-class discussion, hands on, starters, plenary reviews – their answers may give you important feedback on your planning.

Meeting the standards

Some of the discussions you have with colleagues will be related to 'standards'. In England, at the time of writing, you will be expected to show that you have met the Professional Standards for Qualified Teacher Status and Requirements for Initial Teacher Training. Similar standards apply in Wales, with some variation. These standards are grouped around professional values and practice; knowledge and understanding; and teaching. While the details of the standards may change, the framework is expected to remain broadly similar, in the short term at least. At best, the standards approach helps you focus on an aspect of your teaching and points to action in addressing an area to develop; at worst, it results in a tick box procedure with little gain for professional development. To make the standards approach work better for you:

- Try to identify what you do well and where you need to develop for yourself. Then look to see how these aspects of your teaching are described in the Qualified to Teach standards. This will enable you to relate and exemplify the standards to practical experiences in the classroom.
- Discuss with more experienced colleagues what they understand by a standard and, where appropriate, have them model 'good practice' regarding that standard. Ask them for feedback on your attempts to meet that standard, and adapt according to the feedback.
- Try to discuss and observe different approaches to meeting a standard so that you can select what works for you, rather than uncritically following someone else's approach.

CASE STUDY: DEVELOPING YOUR TEACHING DURING TRAINING

Ahmed was enjoying his teaching placement. He was confident in his teaching and felt he was getting good feedback from pupils and colleagues. Most lessons followed a three-part approach – introduction, hands-on activity, and recap. However, he was concerned about how his lessons ended. He would ask pupils to log off and group them around the front of the class while he asked some review questions: what had they achieved that lesson, how could their work be improved, what would they do next lesson? He felt that pupils were reluctant to engage in this kind of review and would have preferred to work at their machines until the end of the lesson. He discussed this with his mentor who suggested more participatory approaches to plenary activities. Ahmed devised simple quizzes in which pupils had to select from four multiple-choice responses. To introduce a game element, pupils had cards with the letters 'a', 'b', 'c' or 'd' written on them which they had to hold up after each question to indicate their choice of answer. A further variation of the game format came when he downloaded a 'Who wants to be a millionaire?' template from the Teachers' Resource Exchange (see Website at the end of this chapter) and set up a quiz show for teams of pupils to take part in. Another approach was to devise a loop game in which cards with a mix of descriptions and key words were handed out to the class. One pupil read a description (for example 'I am a collection of records') for which another pupil held up the key word and announce, say, 'I am a data file'. This pupil would then offer a further description (for example 'I am a collection of fields') for another pupil to recognise. The game would be played until all had taken part. In implementing these strategies, Ahmed was pleased to see that all pupils were now participating in end-of-lesson reviews and he was gaining valuable feedback on what pupils had found difficult in the lesson.

Activity 10.1   An area for development

Identify an area to develop in your teaching. Discuss this with your mentor or with a colleague. Observe how other teachers address this issue and consider possible approaches that you could adopt. Identify how this area for development is represented in the Qualifying to Teach standards.

ADOPTING A LEARNING CYCLE APPROACH

In many cases the development of teaching is not as straightforward as suggested in Ahmed's example. There are several reasons for this. First, it is not always clear where the problem lies. For example what might have been a problem of the plenary in Ahmed's lesson might have really been a problem with the balance between whole-class teaching and hands-on work at machines. Imagine the response of pupils to an end-of-lesson review when a teacher has already given a very long introduction at the start of the lesson. No matter how well-designed the review, pupils are almost bound to feel resentful about being taken away from the computers after waiting so long to access them. More importantly, the purpose of the review is to reflect on the activity and the learning that it has produced; if the activity is foreshortened, there may be little to reflect upon. Second, there is always more than one means of addressing a particular problem. For example, there are many different approaches to plenary activities, some of which might draw better on peer support and group work than those which Ahmed devised. Third, as soon as one problem is addressed another is identified. For example, the plenary activities that Ahmed devised are engaging but may rely heavily on short-term recall and mask pupils' deeper misconceptions. Ahmed might want to extend the range of question types when setting a quiz. Finally, the evaluation of an innovation is rarely clear and cannot solely rely on short-term pupil feedback. For example, many a worthwhile innovation is initially resisted by pupils as it requires a reconsideration of expectations and practice. A more sophisticated model for your professional development is given below (Figure 10.1) which highlights the cyclical nature of learning and a range

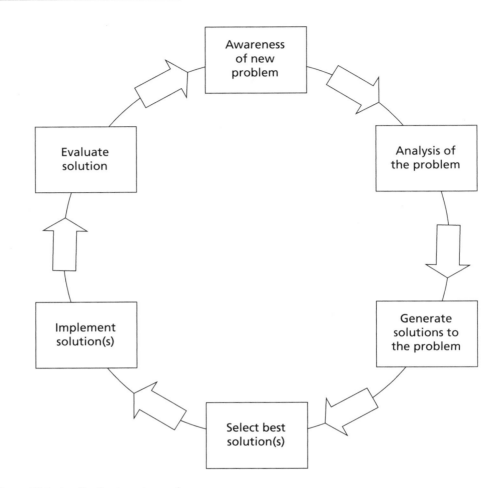

Figure 10.1 A reflective learning cycle

of possible solutions. As an approach, it perhaps resembles aspects of an ICT systems approach.

If he had used a reflective learning cycle approach to planning, Ahmed would have been encouraged to think more deeply about the problem he was trying to address and the different ways in which he might address it. Examples of suggested responses to each stage of the process are given below.

Nature of the problem

- How do I engage pupils in end-of-lesson plenaries?

Analysis

- Is the problem one of too much whole-class work? Are my plenaries too boring for them? Do I lack the presence to stir up classroom debate? Should I forget the more formal end-of-lesson plenary and draw pupils together as a class or a group during the lesson?

Solutions to the problems

- Develop more participatory approaches to the plenary.
- Make introductions to the lesson shorter sharper, more effective.

- Develop more 'just in time' whole-class or small-group teaching interventions while pupils are working at machines.
- NB Get feedback from mentor and colleagues: what do they think?

Select best solution

- Work on different aspects of the problem, but prioritise the most important. This looks like the end of lesson plenary, as this is where I feel most uncomfortable.

Implement

- Devise new approaches to plenary activities.
- NB Make sure I have seen other teachers use these approaches and then start with the classes I am most confident with, and have others watch me.

Evaluation

- Monitor involvement of pupils in the plenary activity. For example, how many contribute, or show signs of interest and engagement?
- NB Make sure I get observed and get feedback from my mentor, and don't rely on pupil feedback.

New problem

- What do the responses to the plenary activities tell me about what pupils find difficult in a topic, and how can I better address the difficulties they experience?

Activity 10.2   Using a reflective learning cycle

Extend your notes from the previous activity to develop a plan for using a reflective learning cycle to address a problem in your teaching.

_____
_____
_____
_____
_____
_____
_____
_____
_____
_____
_____

DEVELOPING YOUR TEACHING AS AN NQT

As an NQT, the context in which you are teaching is different. No matter how inexperienced you may feel, your pupils will be looking at you as a 'proper' teacher, able to deal confidently with their challenges and questions. This makes your job considerably easier if you can quickly adapt to pupils' expectations, but it can lead you to be too eager to go along with existing ways of working and reticent about seeking help from colleagues. Here you might find that a reflective learning cycle approach is again helpful. Remember too that there is considerable support for you as you develop your teaching. For example, you have a reduced teaching timetable, you are not expected to have a tutor group, you are entitled to meetings and feedback on your teaching from your induction tutor and there is generally a local authority-sponsored programme of support for new teachers. The quality of the provision differs. Some schools give a very high priority to supporting new teachers, run excellent programmes in school and encourage new teachers to attend in-service sessions. Other schools leave you to 'sink or swim'. It is clearly important to find out about levels of support before accepting a post. Once in your new school, take advantage of all the help on hand, discuss your needs with your head of department and your induction tutor and be proactive in devising a programme that suits you.

An example of a training programme is provided by one NQT, Corrine. In her first term, Corrine had a particular focus on settling at the school (see Table 10.1). Here she was helped by the training and support offered to all new NQTs through a programme organised by her induction tutor. She was further supported by regular meetings with her head of department (HoD) which enabled her to focus on the teaching of ICT. In one of these meetings she discussed class management. Corrine felt that her management of pupils was good, entry and exit to classrooms was organised and pupils generally listened to her explanations and instructions. Her HoD agreed but asked her to focus on her interactions with pupils while they were working at the machines. This surprised her as she had always felt comfortable with the 'hands-on' stage of the lesson – the pupils were occupied and she was busy ensuring that she helped all pupils get started on the activities she had prepared. However, her HoD asked to her to consider the nature of her interactions with pupils. Very often she was trouble-shooting problems and had little time for one-to-one questioning which would get pupils reflecting on their learning. She also tended to turn away from the class when working with an individual pupil and did not show the 'with-itness' which comes from scanning the class and signalling to pupils that she is aware of all that is going on. Together, Corrine and her HoD discussed ways of better managing pupils at machines and came up with strategies for pupils to assist each other wherever possible. 'Don't ask your teacher before you have asked yourself and your neighbour' became a classroom rule. Corrine developed more awareness of where to position herself when working one-to-one and was careful to circulate the whole room and observe each pupil at least once at some point during the lesson.

Table 10.1 Selected events in Corrine's development programme for her first term

Week	Activity	Focus	Action
1	Meeting with HoD	Review of subject knowledge in teaching new classes	Attend in-service training provided by exam board
			Work through Control software
3	Meeting with induction tutor	Generic issues in class management	Identification of teachers to observe
			Observation schedule of teaching designed
5	Formal observation of lesson by induction tutor	Classroom management	New strategies for intervening while pupils work at machines
7	Observation of other ICT teachers	Use of questioning	Adopt different types of questions in my teaching
9	Team teaching of AS	Comparison of student progress	Adopt more directed approach to course work

In her second term, Corinne had a particular focus on extending her repertoire as a teacher (see Table 10.2). Again she benefited from training events organised at school as well as in-service training organised by the local authority. In addition she found co-mentoring with David, an NQT in the English department whom she had got to know quite well, very helpful. Corrine had been able to support David in developing the use of DTP with his media studies course. In working with David, Corrine saw that he was comfortable with organising pupils into groups and this was something to which they responded well. In contrast, most of Corrine's lessons followed a similar pattern of introduction, hands-on activity, whole-class questioning or plenary review. Her rare attempts to use group work had not been well received by her pupils. David explained that in his department they followed three rules for introducing group work. Each group worked to a tight deadline, no more than 15 or 20 minutes; each member of the group had to contribute at some stage to any discussion; each activity had to result in an identifiable short-term outcome. David and Corrine discussed possible group work activities for her Y12 class. Pupils were organised into groups of four or five and given 20 minutes to script a short role-play on an aspect of health and safety related to the use of ICT. Corrine arranged for David to observe the lesson. The activity was well received, and David and Corrine discussed why this was so and how Corrine could further develop her feedback to pupils at the end of each role-play.

In her third term, Corrine had a particular focus on planning and assessment at Key Stage 3 (see Table 10.3). She had been asked to take on the coordination of the Y7 teaching for next year. She was eager to do this, as she felt the department was still sticking too closely to the KS3 National Strategy for ICT material, which was only meant to exemplify expectations and approaches. As a result, they were missing opportunities to adapt the approach to the needs and interests of their pupils. A second concern was about assessment. Teachers were asked to regularly grade pupils against National Curriculum attainment levels but she was very uncertain if teachers were interpreting these levels in the same way, and she felt that reporting levels to pupils had very little value as they did not understand the criteria by which they were being assessed, nor how they might improve. To address these issues, Corrine arranged to visit ICT departments in other schools. She discovered that some colleagues shared similar concerns but some teachers had contextualised their Y7 teaching better. For example, one school had geared their communicating information work to producing an online guide to the school for Y6 pupils in feeder schools with whom Y7s were in email contact. She also found one school which had used self-assessment regularly at Y7 and had found very 'pupil-friendly' ways to describe different levels of attainment. She was able to take elements of what she saw and use them to update the department's schemes of work. However she was surprised at the resistance of some of her colleagues to change and took care to adapt her ideas to reflect their concerns.

Table 10.2 Selected events in Corrine's development programme for her second term

Week	Activity	Focus	Action
1	Formal observation of lesson by induction tutor	Questioning	Pre-plan different types of questions
3	Visit to colleague from last year's course	Review of concerns in settling in	Sharing of lesson plans and starter activities
5	LEA support group meeting	Review of inclusion strategies	Ensure all teaching material is accessible for pupils with special needs
7	Peer support meetings and observation	Group work	Introduce role-plays to 6th-form teaching

Table 10.3 Selected events in Corrine's development programme for her third term

Week	Activity	Focus	Action
1	Visiting other schools	Planning and assessment at Key Stage 3	Identifying useful ideas and strategies
3	Meeting with colleagues	Planning and assessment	Identifying shared concerns
5	Design new scheme of work	Planning and assessment	Publication for departmental meeting
7	Introducing new scheme of work to the department	Planning and assessment	Amendment following feedback

In looking back at the training events over the year, there were several strengths to Corrine's programme. She was able to draw on a range of sources of support, enabling her to get different perspectives on teaching ICT. She was able to link each development activity to a specific outcome, and the outcomes had practical consequences for her teaching. She was proactive in organising events, such as visits to other schools, which worked for her.

Activity 10.3 When you start as an NQT

You may be reading this chapter some time before you start as an NQT. However, when you do start in your new school, refer back to it and be proactive in devising a development programme of your own, using Corrine's as a guide.

SUMMARY

Your development as a teacher is continuous, from the start of your initial training course, though your induction year and early professional development phase, continuing during your consolidation and accreditation of classroom expertise (perhaps through gaining chartered status or a Master's degree), and into leadership and management training. Having a clear understanding of your objectives and strategies from the beginning will help you to be successful throughout your career.

FURTHER READING

Abbott, I., Bills, E. and Brooks, V. (eds) (2005) *Preparing to Teach*, Buckingham: Open University Press.

Bleach, K. (2000) *The Newly Qualified Secondary Teacher's Handbook*, London: David Fulton.

Capel, S., Leask, M. and Turner, T. (2004) *Starting to Teach in the Secondary School*, London: Routledge.

Cowley, S. (2003) *How to Survive Your First Year in Teaching*, London: Continuum.

Dillon, J. and Maguire, M. (eds) (2001) *Becoming A Teacher: Issues in Secondary Teaching*, Buckingham: Open University Press.

Hammond, M. (2005) *Next Steps in Teaching: A Guide to Your Career as a Secondary Teacher*, London: Routledge.

Thody, A., Gray, B. and Bowden, D. (2000) *The Teacher's Survival Guide*, London: Continuum.

Marland, M. (2002) *The Craft of the Classroom*, London: Heinemann.

WEBSITE

Teachers' Resource Exchange: tre.ngfl.gov.uk.

Appendix A Planning templates

EXAMPLE MEDIUM-TERM UNIT PLAN TEMPLATE

Class:		No. of weeks/hours:	
Scheme of work/syllabus reference:		Unit/topic: Using ICT	
No. in class:	M/F:		SEN:
Comments/prior knowledge:			
Aims: At the end of this unit 1. most pupils will: 2. some pupils will not have made so much progress and will: 3. some pupils will have progressed further and will: Language/literacy: pupils will understand, use and spell correctly:			
Health and safety issues:			

Lesson/wb:	Activities:	Outcomes:	Resources needed:
1			
2			
3			
4			

EXAMPLE MEDIUM-TERM UNIT PLAN

Class: **7 B**		No. of weeks/hours: **4 hours/weeks**	
Scheme of work/syllabus reference: **QCA unit 1.**		Unit/topic: **Using ICT**	
No. in class: **22**	M/F: **12/10**		SEN: **0**
Comments/prior knowledge: **First unit – need to establish prior knowledge. Some will have done multimedia at KS2**			

Aims: At the end of this unit

1. most pupils will: **use slideshow presentation software to organise, refine and present a presentation, with images, sound and text**.
2. some pupils will not have made so much progress and will: **produce a shorter presentation, with images, sound and text**
3. some pupils will have progressed further and will: **have done the presentation, matched it to audience, used buttons and done some in French.**

Language/literacy: Pupils will understand, use and spell correctly: **log on/off, multimedia, plagiarism, button, hyperlink**

Health and safety issues:
Use of whiteboard and projector. Fix cables.

Lesson/wb:	Activities:	Outcomes:	Resources needed:
1 **13 Sept**	1. **See demo of software, how to insert text, graphics and sound** 2. **Plan presentation (storyboard)**	1. **Improved knowledge on software** 2. **Storyboard**	**Whiteboard, slideshow presentation software, blank paper, pencils, rulers**
2 **20 Sept**	1. **Begin slides, save with sensible names, save drafts**	1. **Draft set of slides**	**Network, presentation software, microphones, speakers, scanner, digital camera**
3 **27 Sept**	1. **Finish presentation** 2. **Print as annotated handout** 3. **Plan presentation**	**Finished presentation** **Annotated handouts**	**As above** **Printer** **Paper**
4 **3 Oct**	1. **Make presentation**	**Presentation**	**Presentation software, whiteboard**

EXAMPLE LESSON PLAN TEMPLATE 1

Class:	Date: Venue:	Time:	No. in class: M/F:	Identify least able: Identify most able: Other:
Theme of module:		Theme of lesson:		SOW/NC ref. and level:

Prior learning/notes/errors and misconceptions from last lesson:

Anticipated errors and misconceptions to address this lesson:

Aims (expected learning outcomes) for lesson:

LEAST ABLE PUPILS:	ALL OTHER PUPILS:	MOST PUPILS:	SOME PUPILS:	MOST ABLE PUPILS:

Targeted cross-curricular content, e.g. Literacy, Numeracy, Citizenship, SMSC, study skills, thinking skills, key skills, economic awareness, other subject:

Keywords & literacy support:

Methods of differentiation, e.g. open-ended tasks, increased levels of difficulty, differentiated input, differentiated tasks, teacher support/intervention, class assistant support/intervention, peer support/collaboration, streaming, setting, friendship groups, mixed ability groups, IEP strategies:

Assessment method for aims and outcomes, e.g. Q&A, written task, test, homework, observation, printout:		Recording methods, e.g. mark book, printout, observation notes, Q&A notes, report:

TIMINGS	TEACHER ACTIVITY Intro:	PUPIL ACTIVITY (including differentiation):	RESOURCES: :	ASSESSMENT
	Development:			
	Plenary:			

EXTENSION/HOMEWORK:

TTA Standards:

EXAMPLE LESSON PLAN TEMPLATE 2

(Lesson plan)				Qualification title:	Group ID: Tutor:
No. in class	SEN	Support	Date:	Time:	Topic:
Standards		Theme of module:			Theme of lesson:
Learning objective(s)					
Learning outcomes					

Cross-curricular IDENTIFIED ✓

Literacy	Numeracy	Information Technology	Working with others	Citizenship	SMSC	Listening/thinking skills
TIME	**ACTIVITY**	**LEARNING & TEACHING METHOD**	**RESOURCES**	**Differentiation**	**KEY SKILLS**	**ASSESSMENT**

Extension:

Evaluation:

General issues:

Standards:
Outcomes:
Next lesson:

EXAMPLE LESSON PLAN TEMPLATE 3

Class Week	Date Time	Ability range	No. in the class No. SEN/IEP
Curriculum ref.	Topic		Cross-curricular links

Prior learning

Aims:

Objectives:
All pupils
Most pupils
Some pupils

Key concepts / vocabulary

Differentiation

By open-ended tasks	By differentiated input/tasks	By increasing levels of difficulty	Mixed ability
Teacher support/ intervention	Classroom assistant	Peer support/ collaboration	Streaming
Setting	Friendship groups		

Assessment

Purpose – diagnostic	Formative	Summative	

Method

Question / answer	Written task	Written test	Observation

Recording

Mark book	Report	School data	Observation notes	Pupil / parent

Risk assessment
Pupils to enter and exit room in an orderly manner.
Awareness of trailing cables. No bags in the classroom.
Main pupil activity
Homework

Standards addressed

Class teacher signature if discussed.

Time	Learning/Pupils' activity	Teacher activity	Learning outcomes and assessment

Issues from the previous week:

KS3 EXAMPLE LESSON PLAN

Class: **Y8**	Date: Venue:	Time:	No. in class: **24** M/F: **0/24**	Identify least able: **G1** Identify most able: **G5** Other:
Theme of module: **control & monitoring**		Theme of lesson: **sensing and control**		SOW/NC ref and level: **unit 7.6 level 4/5**

Prior learning/notes/errors and misconceptions from last lesson: **Pupils missed a week due to pastoral session , likely to be lively this lesson**

Anticipated errors and misconceptions to address this lesson: **Entering the web addresses incorrectly & then assuming site does not web**

Aims (expected learning outcomes) for lesson:

LEAST ABLE PUPILS:	ALL OTHER PUPILS:	MOST PUPILS:	SOME PUPILS:	MOST ABLE PUPILS:
G1 and G2 will use guide to answer questions on sensors and control, with teacher support.	**Will use guide to answer questions on sensors and control with relevant additional info from websites, with teacher support.**	**Will use guide to answer questions on sensors and control with relevant additional info from websites, working independently. Use answers to help wordprocess a report.**	**Will use guide to answer questions on worksheet with relevant additional info from websites, working independently. Use the different sources to synthesise answers to help wordprocess an accurate and appropriate report.**	**G5, possibly G7 will use guide to answer questions on worksheet with relevant additional info from websites, working independently. Use synthesis of answers to help wordprocess an accurate and appropriate report. They will be able to justify their conclusions.**

Targeted cross-curricular content, e.g. Literacy, Numeracy, Citizenship, SMSC, study skills (bkxi), thinking skills, key skills (post 16), economic awareness, other subject: **Literacy (reports). Social & economic awareness.**

Keywords & literacy support: **Sensors, control, system flowchart, automation**

Methods of differentiation, e.g. open-ended tasks, increased levels of difficulty, differentiated input, differentiated tasks, teacher support/intervention, class assistant support/intervention, peer support/collaboration, streaming, setting, friendship groups, mixed ability groups, IEP strategies: **Learning styles (VAK) & differentiated input**

Assessment method for aims and outcomes, e.g. Q&A, written task, test, homework, observation, printout: **Printouts and written tasks/worksheet**	Recording methods, e.g. mark book, printout, observation notes, Q&A notes, report: **Mark book**

TIMINGS	TEACHER ACTIVITY	PUPIL ACTIVITY (including differentiation):	RESOURCES: **Music watch**	ASSESSMENT:
5 mins	Intro: **Bring in class to calming music, use hook-up brain gym exercises**	**AK sit, listen and do exercises**		
5 mins	Development: **Clearly state the objectives. Into sense & control, discuss what pupils believe it is, use example of greenhouse to demo how sensors detect temp. & humidity.**	**A** listen to objectives **V** watch PowerPoint during discussion.	**PowerPoint**	**Informal observations, Q&A**
5 mins	**Give pupils instructions for worksheet task, explain only to use websites provided and not misuse internet.** **Check understanding.** **Monitor and support pupils, target weaker pupils throughout. Record progress I markbook.**	**A** listen to instructions.	**Sense and control worksheet**	
30 mins		**V, K Answer the questions, using websites to expand answers. Some will then wordprocess a report, including relevant images and print.**	**Internet, pre-defined websites, markbook**	**Answers, reports**
15 mins	Plenary: **Put pupils into predetermined groups of 4 (6 groups). Give each group one question to brainstorm and feedback.**	**V A use keywords to inform discussion, listen to others.**	**Keywords, coloured pens**	**Written notes**

EXTENSION/HOMEWORK: **use the 'funderstanding' website to control a roller coaster**

TTA Standards: **3.2.2, 3.3.8**

KS4 EXAMPLE LESSON PLAN (COURSEWORK)

Class: **Y10 vocational**	Date: Venue:	Time:	No. in class: **21** M/F: **10/11**	Identify least able: **B1** Identify most able: **G2, G3 & B5** Other:

Theme of module: **Vocational coursework**	Theme of lesson: **unit 3 – Hardware & software, unit 7 – multimedia**	SOW/NC ref and level: **units 3 & 7 pass/merit**

Prior learning/notes/errors and misconceptions from last lesson:
B1, G4, B7, B9, G11 still finishing unit 3, others have begun unit 7

Anticipated errors and misconceptions to address this lesson:
Some are simply copying & pasting images from internet, rather than saving to folder then inserting image – will remind them to use folders

Aims (expected learning outcomes) for lesson:

LEAST ABLE PUPILS:	ALL OTHER PUPILS:	MOST PUPILS:	SOME PUPILS:	MOST ABLE PUPILS:
B1, G4 to complete unit 3 at pass level.	**B7, B9, G11 to complete unit 3 and start unit 7. Working independently for some of time at pass level.**	**Start unit 7. Working independently for the majority of time at pass level.**	**Making progress on unit 7. Working independently for the majority of time at merit level.**	**G2, G3, B5 to make significant progress on unit 7. Working independently for at merit level.**

Targeted cross-curricular content, e.g. Literacy, Numeracy, Citizenship, SMSC, study skills (bkxi), thinking skills, key skills (post 16), economic awareness, other subject:
Literacy – writing for a specific audience. Key skills – communication with peers. Thinking skills. Economic awareness – ICT in industry.

Keywords & literacy support:
Graphics, hardware, software, internet, research, evaluation, screen shot

Methods of differentiation, e.g. open-ended tasks, increased levels of difficulty, differentiated input, differentiated tasks, teacher support/intervention, class assistant support/intervention, peer support/collaboration, streaming, setting, friendship groups, mixed ability groups, IEP strategies:
differentiated support through guides and teacher intervention. Peer support.

Assessment method for aims and outcomes, e.g. Q&A, written task, test, homework, observation, printout: **Planned Q&A, teacher notes**	Recording methods, e.g. mark book, printout, observation notes, Q&A notes, report:

TIMINGS	TEACHER ACTIVITY	PUPIL ACTIVITY (including differentiation):	RESOURCES:	ASSESSMENT:
10 mins	Intro: **Register. Share lesson objectives. Demo on using folders for images.**	**Get folders, log on.** **Interact with demo Q & A.**	**Register, PCs projector**	**Q & A**
36 mins	Development: **Monitoring class, facilitation of coursework, supporting pupils.**	**Working through unit tasks, with support of guides.**		**Targeted Q & A**

| 9 mins | Plenary:
Q & A on using images, considering technical issues, appropriateness of images and copyright laws. | **Respond to Q & A.** | **Planned Q & A** |
| | **Supervised ending.** | **Pack up.** | |

EXTENSION/HOMEWORK: **Extension – next unit tasks available.**

TTA Standards: **2.1 d, 3.3.2d Awareness of pathways of progression**

POST-16 EXAMPLE LESSON PLAN

Class: **12Y**	Date: Venue:	Time: **60mins**	No. in class: **11** M/F: **7/4**	Identify least able: **G1** Identify most able: **B3 and G5** Other:
Theme of module: **Multimedia**		Theme of lesson: **Evaluating websites**		SOW/NC ref and level: **AVCE Unit 3.7**

Prior learning/notes/errors and misconceptions from last lesson: **Majority have undertaken GCSE ICT examination in KS4. All have been engaged in initial discussion on their experiences of using the internet**

Anticipated errors and misconceptions to address this lesson: **Not evaluating all features of a website, particularly design and content and ease of use. Lack of understanding of the needs of target audience**

Aims (expected learning outcomes) for lesson:

LEAST ABLE PUPILS:	ALL OTHER PUPILS:	MOST PUPILS:	SOME PUPILS:	MOST ABLE PUPILS:
B3 and G5 Determine some criteria for the evaluation a website. Use a standardised list to undertake a meaningful evaluation of a website.		**Determine suitable criteria for the evaluation a website. Use these criteria in conjunction with a standardised list to undertake meaningful evaluation of more than one website.**		**G1 Determine suitable criteria for the evaluation of a website. Use these criteria to undertake meaningful evaluation of a variety of websites and begin to apply these findings to the design of their own website.**

Targeted cross-curricular content, e.g. Literacy, Numeracy, Citizenship, SMSC, study skills (bkxi), thinking skills, key skills (post 16), economic awareness, other subject: **Thinking skills and economic and social awareness**

Keywords & literacy support: **Navigation, bias, fitness for purpose, target audience, design features, credibility and validity, accuracy, reliability**

Methods of differentiation, e.g. open-ended tasks, increased levels of difficulty, differentiated input, differentiated tasks, teacher support/intervention, class assistant support/intervention, peer support/collaboration, streaming, setting, friendship groups, mixed ability groups, IEP strategies: **Group work, peer support and appropriate teacher intervention**

Assessment method for aims and outcomes, e.g. Q&A, written task, test, homework, observation, printout: **Q and A and feedback from students**	Recording methods, e.g. mark book, printout, observation notes, Q&A notes, report: **Observational notes**

TIMINGS	TEACHER ACTIVITY	PUPIL ACTIVITY (including differentiation):	RESOURCES:	ASSESSMENT:
	Intro:			
2 mins	**Registration.**		**Register**	
1 min	**Share lesson objectives.**		**Whiteboard**	
7 mins	**Introduce starter activity.** **Monitor discussion.**	**In groups (at least 3 per group). Identify good and bad points of exemplar websites.**	**PowerPoint** **Flip chart**	**Feedback**
5 mins	**Manage feedback.**	**Group feedback.**		
5 mins	Development: **Introduce standarised list of criteria.**	**Discuss list.**	**Interactive whiteboard Criteria list on shared area**	**Q and A**
5 mins	**Reinforce the concepts of fitness for purpose and needs of target audience.**	**Respond to targeted questions.**		
3 mins	**Provide list of sites for pupils to evaluate.**	**Investigate sites. C3 and C5 to identify and evaluate additional sites.**	**Internet access**	
22 mins	Plenary: **Manage discussion about finds.**	**Participate in debate** **C1 to scribe findings on Smart Board and save in shared area**	**Interactive whiteboard**	**Observational notes**

EXTENSION/HOMEWORK: **Begin to apply findings to the design of own website**

TTA Standards:
2.1d Awareness of pathways of progression
3.2.4 Differentiation
3.3.2d Teach competently

Appendix B   Examples of simple peer- and self-assessment tools

PEER-ASSESSMENT

Y7 Group presentations – feedback sheet						
Group	1	2	3	4	5	6
Readable font	Y					
Images	Y					
Animation	N					
Sound	Y					
Colour	Y					
Comment	Liked the colour, but sound did not match the images.					

SELF-ASSESSMENT

Group	Yes/no	Explain
Are my fonts clear and readable?	Yes	They are in Arial size 24.
Are the images suitable for the audience?	Y	My audience is Y6, so I have used cartoons.
Have I used animation?	N	
Have I used sound?	Y	
Are the colour combinations suitable?	Y	

Appendix C

Reports for newsroom simulation

MESSAGE 1

There has been a mid-air collision between an RAF jet and a helicopter. It is believed that all passengers have been killed.

MESSAGE 2

A helicopter pilot and two passengers were killed instantly today at 2.00 p.m. when an RAF jet hit his aircraft at 600mph.

MESSAGE 3

Emergency services at Kendal have been called to the scene of an air crash near a primary school. Two people have been killed.

MESSAGE 4

Mavis Bainbridge, of West View Farm, Crooklands, near to the crash scene, said: 'We do have RAF Tornados swooping low over our house and farm almost every day, and sometimes they do look as though they will hit the farm'.

MESSAGE 5

Helicopter pilot Robert Reid (35) and Alan Trucker (52) died instantly as their Bell Jet Ranger crashed into a farmyard just south of Kendal, Cumbria. They were working for Shell Oil inspecting a pipeline near Kendal, Cumbria.

MESSAGE 6

The jet, an RAF Tornado was practising low-level bombing runs.

MESSAGE 7

The damaged jet, which had been flying at 385 mph, made an emergency landing at the British Aerospace factory at Warton, near Preston. The crew of the jet said that they thought that they had flown into a flock of birds and knew nothing of the collision with the Bell 206B Jet Ranger.

MESSAGE 8

Both aircraft were undertaking routine operations and it is assumed that flight plans would have been filed. Investigators for an RAF board of inquiry and the Department of Transport's air accident investigation bureau are at the scene of the crash at present, searching for clues into the cause of the accident.

MESSAGE 9

Two bodies have been taken from the wreckage of a Bell helicopter which crashed in flames near Kendal.

MESSAGE 10

Cumbria County Council's deputy leader John Whiteman said: 'We have warned for a long time that low flying in the region has been an accident waiting to happen. We want stricter guidelines and further assurances that something like this can never happen again.'

MESSAGE 11

The Ministry of Defence report that, one of a pair from RAF Bruggen in Germany, the Tornado left RAF Bruggen on a routine training flight, including low-level flying in the Lake District. It is believed that it had been flying at 380 mph at a height of 500ft.

MESSAGE 12

Air traffic control at Warton near Preston say that at the time of the crash, the trace for the helicopter disappeared after its path crossed the RAF jet. The Ministry of Defence report that one engine of the jet is badly damaged.

MESSAGE 13

The Tornado landed safely at the British Aerospace airfield at Warton, in Preston, suffering severe damage to its front carriage. A Ministry of Defence spokesman reports that neither the pilot or navigator were injured.

MESSAGE 14

Air traffic control at Warton near Blackpool had no radio contact with the helicopter after 11.15 a.m. Radar contact was lost shortly before noon.

MESSAGE 15

Helicopter crew Mr Reid, (37) from Chirnside, Berwickshire and his wife Carol (32) were expecting their second child next month. They have a 15-month-old son. Mr Tucker (55) an Area Superintendent with Shell Chemicals UK, had been carrying out an inspection of the North Ethylene Pipeline at the time. He had worked with Shell for thirty-four years and was due to retire next year. He was the father of three adult sons and a grandfather of seven children.

MESSAGE 16

Near misses between civilian aircraft and RAF jets are becoming more common. The shadow Defence Minister is going to raise the incident in the Commons. He said: 'This underlies the dangers of low flying. Low flying, however important for RAF training, must not be allowed to endanger civilian life. There is a constant fear that major accidents are just waiting to happen.'

MESSAGE 17

Mrs Gillian Robinson, walking her dog in a nearby village saw the helicopter spiralling out of control. 'I just looked up because there were some jets flying over and then I looked over and saw the helicopter. It was just going round and round – it was falling out of the sky.'

MESSAGE 18

An air traffic controller, who did not wish to be named, said: There is little liaison between the RAF and civilian air traffic control. Near misses are quite common.

MESSAGE 19

The accident scattered wreckage over a wide area, close to Junction 36 of the M6 near Kirkby Lonsdale.

MESSAGE 20

A close relative of one of the dead men said he could not believe that the Tornado crew did not know they had hit the helicopter. He accused the RAF of a cover-up.

MESSAGE 21

Mavis Bainbridge of West View Farm, near the crash scene said: 'We have RAF planes swooping low over the house almost every day. Sometimes they look as if they are going to hit the farm. The animals get very upset sometimes. Last week our hens stopped laying because of the noise of the jets.'

MESSAGE 22

The Defence Secretary denied that the crash could have been avoided if the ALFENS (Automatic Low Flying Entry and Planning Notification System) safety system had been introduced. There has already been a serious delay in introducing this system and under the present system of radio contact and paper charts there is a continuing risk of disastrous accidents.

Bibliography

Adey, P. and Shayer, M. (1994) *Really Raising Standards: Cognitive Intervention and Academic Achievement*, London: Routledge.

BBC (2005) *Nasa probe strikes Comet Tempel 1*, London: BBC. Available at <http://news.bbc.co.uk/2/hi/science/nature/4647673.stm> (accessed 18 July 2005).

Becta (2002) *The Impact of ICT on Pupil Learning and Attainment*, Coventry: Becta.

Birmingham Grid for Learning (2005) *Glossary*, Birmingham: Birmingham Grid for Learning. Available at <http://www2.bgfl.org/bgfl2/learning/glossary.cfm?zz=20050227150330> (accessed 15 March 2005).

Black, P. and Wiliam, D. (1998) *Inside the Black Box*, London: Assessment Reform Group.

Bruner, J. (1996) *The Culture of Education*, Cambridge, MA: Harvard University Press.

Capel, S., Leask, M. and Turner, T. (2005) *Learning to Teach in the Secondary School* (third edn), London: RoutledgeFalmer.

Child, D. (1997) *Psychology and the Teacher*, London: Cassell.

Cowley, S. (2003), *Getting the Buggers to Behave 2*, London: Continuum.

Craft, A. (2001) 'Little c creativity.' In Craft, A., Jeffrey, B. and Leibling, M. (eds) *Creativity in Education*, London: Continuum.

Csikszentmihalyi, M. (1996) *Creativity: Flow and the Psychology of Discovery and Invention*, New York: HarperCollins.

De Bono, E. (1996) *Teach Yourself to Think*, London: Penguin.

DfEE (1997) *Connecting the Learning Society*, London: DfEE.

DfEE (1999) *The National Curriculum*, London: DfEE.

DfES (2002) *Sample Teaching Units for ICT – Year 7*, London: DfES. Available at <http://www.standards.dfes.gov.uk/keystage3/respub/ictsampley7> (accessed 14 June 2005).

DfES (2003) *KS3 Strategy, Foundation Subjects Strand: Key Messages about Assessment for Learning*, London: DFES. Available at <http://www.standards.dfes.gov.uk/keystage3/downloads/fs_km_afl004503.pdf> (accessed 14 June 2005).

DfES (2004a) *Securing Level 5 in ICT*, London: DfES. Available at <http://www.standards.dfes.gov.uk/keystage3/downloads/ict_securingl5_booklet.pdf> (accessed 14 June 2005).

DfES (2004b) *Whole School Development in Assessment for Learning*, London: DfES. Available at <http://www.standards.dfes.gov.uk/keystage3/respub/afl_ws> (accessed 14 June 2005).

DfES (2004c) *Key Stage 3 National Strategy Pedagogy and Practice Unit 12: Assessment for Learning*, London: DfES. Available at <http://www.standards.dfes.gov.uk/keystage3/respub/sec_pptl0> (accessed 9 June 2005).

DfES (2004d) *Leading in Learning: Developing Thinking Skills at Key Stage 3*, London: DfES. Available at <http://www.standards.dfes.gov.uk/keystage3/downloads/ws_lil_ts003605slead.pdf> (accessed 14 June 2005).

DfES (2004e) *ICT across the Curriculum*, London: DfES. Available at <http://www.standards. dfes.gov.uk/keystage3/respub/ictac> (accessed 9 June 2005).

DfES (2004f) *Leading in Learning: Exemplification in ICT*, London: DfES. Available at <http://www.standards.dfes.gov.uk/keystage3/respub/ws_lil_ts> (accessed 12 July 2005).

DfES (2004g) *Key Stage 3 National Strategy: Literacy and Learning in ICT*, London: DfES. Available at <http://www.standards.dfes.gov.uk/keystage3/respub/ws_lal> (accessed 12 July 2005).

DfES (2004h) *Principles for Constructing a Scheme of Work*, London DfES. Available at <www.standards.dfes.gov.uk/schemes2/secondary_ICT/principles> (accessed 9 November 2006).

DfES (2005a) *What is Assessment?* London: DfES. Available at <http://www.standards.dfes.gov.uk/primary/features/primary/1091819/1092063> (accessed 12 July 2005).

DfES (2005b) *Personalised Learning*, London: DfES. Available at <http://www.standards.dfes.gov.uk/personalisedlearning> (accessed 23 December 2005).

Elliott, P. (2004) 'Planning for learning'. In Brooks V., Abbott I. and Bills, L. (eds) *Preparing to Teach in Secondary Schools*, Buckingham: Open University Press.

Gamble, N. and Easingwood, N. (2000) *ICT and Literacy: Information and Communications Technology, Media, Reading and Writing*, London: Continuum.

Grinter, R. and Eldridge, M. (2001) 'y do tngrs luv 2 txt msg?'. In Prinz, W. Jarke, M., Rogers, Y., Schmidt, K. and Wulf, V. (eds): *Proceedings of the Seventh European Conference on Computer Supported Cooperative Work ECSW '01, Bonn, Germany*, Dordrecht, Netherlands: Kluwer Academic Publishers: 219–238.

Jarvis, P. (2004) *Adult Education and Lifelong Learning: Theory and Practice*, London: RoutledgeFalmer.

Kennewell, S., Parkinson, J. and Tanner, H. (eds) (2003) *Learning to Teach ICT in the Secondary School*, London: RoutledgeFalmer.

Kinchin, G. (2002) 'Learning and learning styles'. In Ellis, V. (ed.) *Learning and Teaching in Secondary Schools*, Exeter: Learning Matters.

Lang, P. (2004) 'Pastoral care and the role of the tutor in preparing to teach in secondary schools'. In Brooks, V., Abbott I. and Bills L. (eds) *Preparing to Teach in Secondary Schools*, Buckingham: Open University Press.

Leask, M. and Younie, S. (2001) 'Communal constructivist theory: information and communications technology pedagogy and internationalisation of the curriculum', *Journal of Information Technology for Teacher Education* 10: 117–134.

Leat, D. (1998) *Thinking Through Geography*, Cambridge: Chris Kington Publishing.

Leat, D. and Higgins, S. (2002) 'The role of powerful pedagogical strategies in curriculum development', *The Curriculum Journal* 13: 71–85.

Lodge, D. (2002) *Thinks*, London: Penguin Books.

Loveless, A. (2002) *Literature Review in Creativity, Technology and Learning*, Bristol: Futurelab. Available at <http://www.futurelab.org.uk/download/pdfs/research/lit_reviews/Creativity-Review.pdf> (accessed 9 November 2006).

Loveless, A. and Wegerif, R. (2004) 'Unlocking creativity with ICT'. In Fisher, R. and Williams, M. (eds) *Unlocking Creativity: Teaching Across the Curriculum*, London: David Fulton.

Lucas, B. (2001) 'Creative teaching, teaching creativity and creative learning'. In Craft, A., Jeffrey, B. and Leibling, M. (eds) (2001) *Creativity in Education*, London: Continuum.

Maslow, M. (1970) *Motivation and Personality*, London, Harper and Row.

Matthewman, S. and Trigg, P. (2004) 'Obsessive compulsive font disorder: the challenge of supporting pupils writing with the computer', *Computers and Education* 43: 125–135.

NACCCE (1999) *All our Futures: Creativity, Culture and Education*, London: DfEE.

Netiquette (2005) *Netiquette Home Page*. Available at <www.albion.com/netiquette> (accessed 14 June 2005).

Ofsted (2004) *Ofsted Subject Reports 2002/03: Information and Communication Technology in*

Secondary Schools, London: Ofsted. Available at <http://www.ofsted.gov.uk/publications/index.cfm?fuseaction=pubs.summary&id=3540> (accessed 15 March 2005).

Oxford Paperback Dictionary (1994) Oxford: Oxford University Press.

Pollard, A. (2005) *Reflective Teaching* (second edn), London: Continuum.

Polya, G. (1963) 'On learning, teaching, and learning teaching', *The American Mathematical Monthly* 70: 605–619.

Prashnig, B. (2006) *Learning Styles and Personalised Teaching*, London: Continuum.

QCA (2005) 'What is creativity?' Available at <http://www.ncaction.org.uk/creativity/whatis.htm> (accessed 15 June 2005).

Resnick, L. (1987) *Education and Learning to Think,* Washington, DC: National Academy Press.

Sargeant, J. (1995) 'What is the range of writing?' In Protherough, R. and King, P. (eds) *The Challenge of English in the National Curriculum*, London: Routledge.

Scriven, M. (1970) 'Philosophy of education: learning theory and teaching machines', *The Journal of Philosophy* 67: 896–908.

Sewell, D. (1990) *New Tools for New Minds,* New York: Harvester Wheatsheaf.

Stephens, P. and Crawley, T. (2002) *Becoming an Effective Teacher*, Cheltenham: Nelson Thornes.

Truss, L. (2003) *Eats, Shoots & Leaves,* London: Profile Books.

TTA (1998) *The Use of ICT in Subject Teaching: Expected Outcomes for Teachers*, London: Teacher Training Agency and the Department of Education.

Ultralab (2005) *What is M learning?* Chelmsford: Ultralab. Available at <http://www.m-learning.org/index.shtml> (accessed 23 December 2005).

Vygotsky, L. S. (1978) *Mind in Society: The Development of Higher Psychological Processes*, Cambridge, MA: Harvard University Press.

Webb, M. (2002) 'Pedagogical reasoning: issues and solutions for the teaching and learning of ICT in secondary schools', *Education and Information Technologies* 7: 237–255.

Webb, M. (2005) 'Affordances of ICT in science learning: implications for an integrated pedagogy', *International Journal of Science Education* 27: 705–735.

Wheeler, S. (2005) *Transforming Primary ICT,* Exeter: Learning Matters.

Wikipedia (2005a) *Exploration.* Available at <http://en.wikipedia.org/wiki/Exploration> (accessed 18 July 2005).

Wikipedia (2005b) *Christopher Columbus.* Available at <http://en.wikipedia.org/wiki/Christopher_Columbus> (accessed 18 July 2005).

Wikipedia (2005c) *James Cook.* Available at <http://en.wikipedia.org/wiki/James_Cook> (accessed 18 July 2005).

Wikipedia (2005d) *Space Exploration.* Available at <http://en.wikipedia.org/wiki/Space_Exploration> (accessed 18 July 2005).

Wikipedia (2005e) *Information Overload.* Available at <http://en.wikipedia.org/wiki/Information_overload> (accessed 18 July 2005).

Williams, L. (2005) *Video-conferencing in Schools.* Available at http://www.mirandanet.dial.pipex.com/ftp/lwilliams5.pdf (accessed 14 June 2005).

Index